BEVERLY HIGH FOOTBALL IN THE TWENTIETH CENTURY

It was our intent to create a chronicle, in mostly pictorial form, that would be a collection of interest as well as a fun excursion through all the years of Beverly High football in the Twentieth Century.

We have researched as best we can, yet still some team pictures and pictures of players were not to be found and, in fact, some of the pictures are not good quality and some are a bit fuzzy, but we felt the players that were involved deserved to be included.

We envision it to be a joyful search through all those years to find our sons, brothers, fathers, uncles, grandfathers and, yes, even some great-grandfathers that all expended the very same effort, experienced the same difficulties, tasted the same bitterness of defeat, as well as the overwhelming joy in the teamwork of winning. It matters not that it be 1900 or 1999, the joy and sense of accomplishment is shared by all of those who participated in the sport of football.

Charlie Walsh once aptly said that the game of football made men of teenagers. This is a chronicle as well as a tribute to these men.

Please enjoy.

This history of Beverly High School football
was researched and created
by

Sandy Kessaris

Bob Carr

Dick Batchelder

with
an enormous amount of help from all the generous people to whom we are indebted
who enthusiastically shared their memories, their articles and their pictures
to make this book as complete as possible

and
to the following interested organizations:
Beverly High School
Beverly Public Library
Beverly Sports Club
The *Beverly Citizen*
The *Salem Evening News*

and
The Beverly Historical Society
to which all the net profits of this book will be directed

and, finally,
this book ultimately is dedicated to those countless fans
who braved all kinds of weather to support, each year,
the new edition of Beverly High School football.

June 2006

Did you know . . . . .

- that during the early years of its history American football (a spin-off of European soccer and English Rugby) was considered a brutal sport, played without any protective pads or headgear. In fact, at the end of the 1905 season, the Chicago Tribune reported 18 FOOTBALL PLAYERS DEAD AND 159 SERIOUSLY INJURED . . . and prompted President Theodore Roosevelt to proclaim: *"I demand that football change its rules or be abolished. Brutality and foul play should receive the same summary punishment given to a man who cheats at cards! Change the game or forsake it!"*

- that when helmets were first developed, the few to wear the protective device were known as 'sissies'.

- that before standardized rules and regulations were adopted, a team could consist of as many as twenty-five to thirty participants per side and all players played both offense and defense and once the game started, a player could not leave the field unless he was actually injured. As expected, 'faked injuries' became commonplace.

- that the game itself consisted of two 45 minute halves (as in soccer) unless a different time period was agreed upon by both teams.

- that the playing field could be any length or width agreed upon by each team, but was almost always 100 yards or more in length and between 50 and 75 yards wide.

- that the ball originally was a pigs bladder, filled and shaped like an egg and because of its size and ovate shape, it was near impossible to pass successfully. With the change of the ball's size and shape, however, the pass became a valid option for the offense. Unfortunately some officials and coaches frowned on the passing game and, therefore, placed restrictions on it in order to discourage its use, i.e. the pass must travel 5 yards or more past the line of scrimmage and if the pass went incomplete, the team was penalized 15 yards, and catching the ball in the end zone was a touchback, resulting in the defensive team taking possession of the ball on the 20 yard line.

- that originally teams had 3 downs to make 5 yards.

- that until 1882 no yard lines crossed the field to help the referee spot the ball and when the marking of the 5 yard lines was implemented, the football field was called a 'gridiron'.

- that there was no neutral zone between the two scrimmage lines, only an imaginary line drawn through the center of the ball and nearly all linemen lined up squarely against his opponent in an upright position and fought it out with each other, fist and feet.

- that players were permitted to grab hold of their runners any way they could to pull, yank, or push them forward and ball carriers could crawl with the ball until they were held down.

In the beginning . . . . .

1890

Front row, left to right: William Quiner, Doc Dudley, Max Butler, and Dick Woodberry.
Second row, left to right: George Beckford, Chine Bennett, Dick Fraser, H. B. Norwood, William Foster, Arthur Kent, and Cusky Farnham.
In the rear, from left: Lawrence P. Stanton and Ora B. Currier

About 1873, only eight years after the Civil War, the seed was planted that would eventually grow into the first football team in the history of Beverly High School . . . and, as they say, the rest is history.

The football, held by Harry B. Norwood in the center of the rear row, bears little resemblance to the ball of today and, unfortunately, the records of this team are unavailable.

(Note: This picture appeared in the newspaper in 1940. They labeled this team as the 'first' and stated that it was either 1890 or 1891).

1900

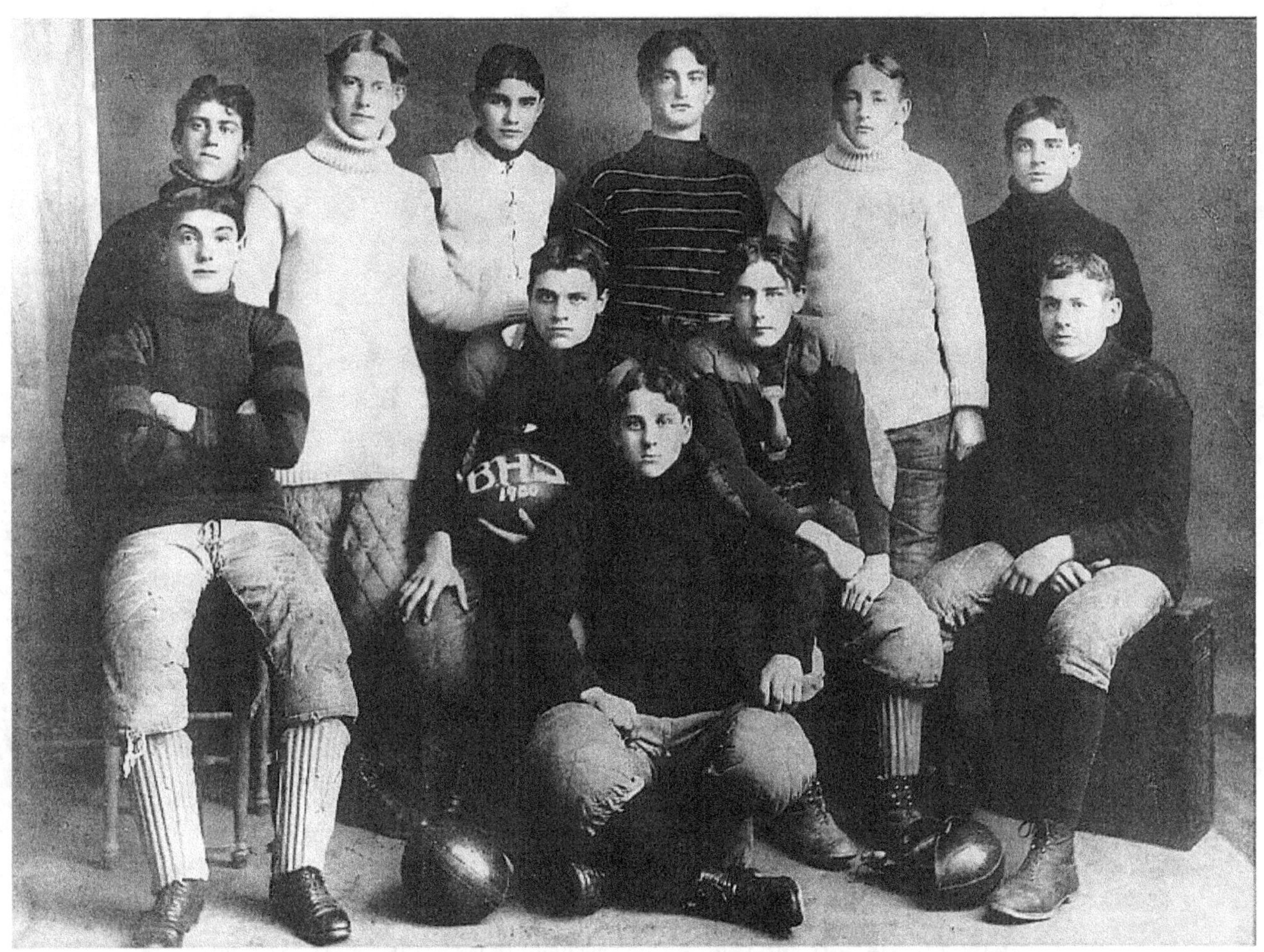

In the front: Ray Webber

Second row: Joe Bonaventura, Jim Fullerton, Roy Walker, Frank Gorman

Back row: Webber, Everett Dodge, Guy Maloon, Ray Jenkins, Bert Wallace, Henry Odell

(Not Pictured)

Captain Harry Guinivan, Littlefield, Ward, Haskell, Broughton, Eaton, Toomey, Bell, Gregg, Tratt, Woodbury, Jones, Wallis

Schedule

Beverly	0	Lynn Classical	12
Beverly	0	Lynn High School	28
Beverly	5	Salem	28
Beverly	0	Salem	11
Beverly	10	Gloucester Y.M.C.A.	0
Beverly	5	Alumni	2

2 – 4 - 0

1901

Team Listing – Does not identify photograph

Littlefield, Allen, Tratt, Hinkley, McLaughlin, Iverson, J.A.Wallace, G.Wallis,
Broughton, Gregg, Williams, Captain J.Fullerton, Coach Crowley, Herrick,
Robertson, Walker, Johnson, Dodge, Callahan, Sullivan, Gorman, Porter

Schedule

Beverly	0		Peabody	0
Beverly	1	(Forfeit)	Peabody	0
Beverly	12		Granite A.A. (Glou'ster)	6
Beverly	0		Thorndike A.A.	5
Beverly	0		Thorndike A.A.	11
Beverly	0		Newburyport	30
Beverly	11		Beverly Farms	5
Beverly	6		South Boston	0
Beverly	11		Columbus A.A.(Glou'str)	10

5 – 3 – 1

1902

Team Listing – Does not identify photograph

Captain James Fullerton, Herrick, Caldwell, Williams, Larcom, Mason, McLaughlin, Smalley, Quigley, Gorman, Wiseman, Robertson, St. Clair, Standley, Whipple, Foster, Iverson, Kent, Raymond, Dodge.

Schedule

Beverly	0	Salem	0
Beverly	5	Danvers	5
Beverly	0	Lynn High	5
Beverly	6	Salem	0
Beverly	21	Gloucester	0
Beverly	5	Peabody	0
Beverly	0	Lincoln A.A.	11
Beverly	5	Lincoln A.A.	0
Beverly	12	Lynn High	0
Beverly	5	M.I.T.	0
Beverly	0	Peabody	5
Beverly	12	Carlton Prep	0
Beverly	0	Danvers	11
Beverly	0	Beverly 1900 Team	0
Beverly	6	Thorndike Club	5

8 – 4 - 3

1903

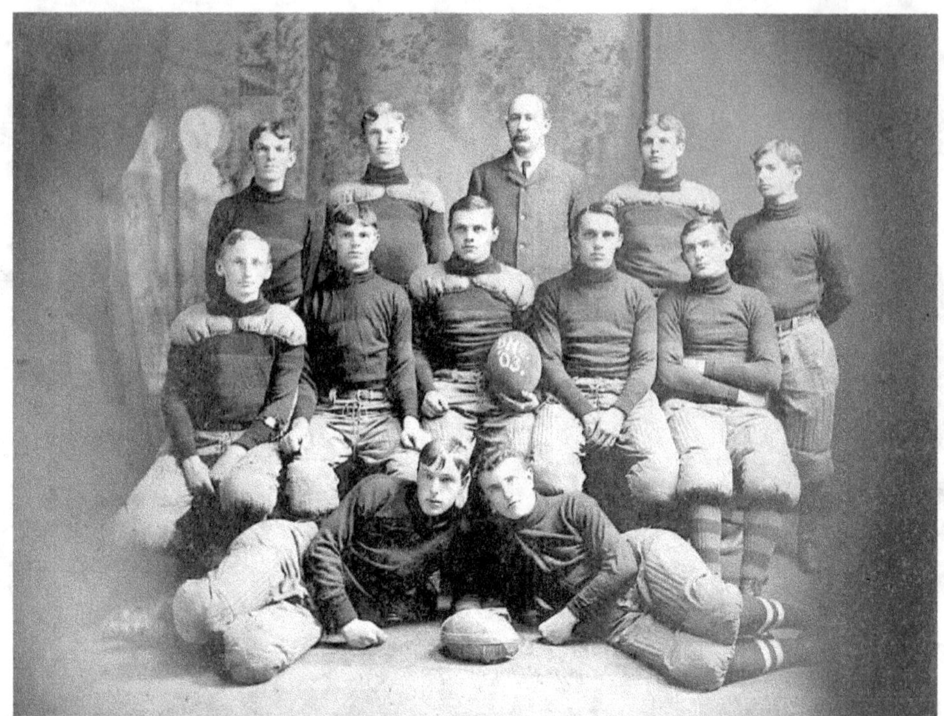

Team Listing – Does not identify photograph

Coach F.W.C. Foster, Captain J. Fullerton, R. Fullerton, C.A. Herrick, M. Kent, A. Wallis, E. Beary, J. Williams, J. Mason, J. Foster, E. Raymond, Quigley, Arnold, Cook, Robertson, Ward, Smith.

Schedule

Beverly	6	Salem	5
Beverly	10	Danvers	5
Beverly	0	Atlantic A.A.	5
Beverly	0	Peabody	0
Beverly	6	Gov. Dummer	6
Beverly	0	Salem	28
Beverly	6	Boston Prep	0
Beverly	23	Peabody	0
Beverly	5	Newburyport	16
Beverly	5	Dorchester	24
Beverly	6	Dummer Academy	6
Beverly	18	Gloucester	11
Beverly	24	Hartford A.A.	0
Beverly	0	Haverhill	18
Beverly	5	Gloucester	0
Beverly	0	Alumni	6

7 – 6 - 3

1904

Team Listing – Does not identify photograph

Coach: Carl Iverson, Arnold, Wallis, Mason, Berry, Williams, Foster, M. Kent, H. Kent, Harrigan, Hayden, R. Fullerton, Ober, McLaughlin, Woodbury, McSweeney, Lewis, McCleary, Maguire, Trowt, Cook, Alley, Larcom, Broughton.

Schedule

Beverly	10	Danvers	11
Beverly	17	Manchester	0
Beverly	0	Gloucester	5
Beverly	6	Dorchester	57
Beverly	5	Salem	0
Beverly	24	Gloucester	0
Beverly	0	Newburyport	5
Beverly	17	Manchester	11
Beverly	0	Mechanical Arts	15
Beverly	0	Gloucester	6
Beverly	5	Danvers	0
Beverly	5	Wakefield	0
Beverly	16	Alumni	0

7 – 6 – 0

1905

Team Listing – Does not identify photograph

Coach Doc Stanley, Captain Fullerton, Wittenhagen, Alley, McIntosh, Berry, Perkins, Larcom, Stevens, Perkins, Willard, Trowt, Hill, Clark, Raymond, Brown, McEachern, Casey, Foster, Kent.

Schedule

Beverly	5	Lawrence	5
Beverly	0	Mechanical Arts	11
Beverly	12	Danvers	0
Beverly	10	Alumni	0
Beverly	16	Gloucester	6
Beverly	28	Chelsea	0
Beverly	23	Salem	0
Beverly	22	Gloucester	6
Beverly	5	Danvers	0
Beverly	5	Haverhill	16
Beverly	23	U.S.S. Enterprise	0
Beverly	6	Gloucester	22
Beverly	18	Danvers	0
Beverly	0	Salem	0

9 – 3 – 2

1906

First row: Young boy not identified

Second row: Coach: B. H. 'Beet' Squires, D.McEachern, Pierce, O. Willard, M. Kent, Manager.

Third row: W. Hayden, J. Raymond, T. Casey, Captain H. Perkins, J. Stevens.

Fourth row: F. Wittenhagen, H. Kent, E. Blanchard.

Other players not shown: Carleton, Quigley, Wallis, Riddle, Jones, Brown, Kelleher, Pepper, Hodge

Schedule

Beverly	0	Lawrence	0
Beverly	0	South Boston	6
Beverly	16	Saugus	0
Beverly	6	Medford	0
Beverly	0	Haverhill	11
Beverly	0	Mechanical Arts	0
Beverly	10	Danvers	0
Beverly	6	Roxbury	0
Beverly	0	Everett	4
Beverly	28	Gloucester	2
Beverly	5	Salem	0

6 – 3 – 2

1907

Coach: B. H. 'Beet' Squires

Team

R. Trask, R. Cooney, Fred Wallis, Jesse Stevens, William Hayden, Hill,
Fred Whittenhagan, R.T. Carleton, Thomas Casey, Fred Cann, Raymond,
A. Connolly, E. Brown, Fullerton, Tratt, Iverson, Broughton, R. Dodge,
W. Dodge, R. Tarr, J. Kelleher, C. Crosby, C. Ward, G. Standley.

INTERESTING NOTES

- The names of the players were placed on the bulletin board, and a careful record was made of each of their subjects, and those that dropped below the standard handed in their suits until all back work was made up.

- The home games were played on Beverly Common.

- The first game of the season was scheduled for Saturday, Sept. 28 at Lawrence. The team traveled as far as Danvers when word was received that Lawrence could not play.

- The Lowell game was held up due to a train delay from Lowell to Beverly.

- The Waltham game was not originally scheduled and was played after the Thanksgiving Day game with Salem and the players were not prepared.

- It was noted in the Aegis that although the attendance at the games was very good, there had been little cheering and they requested 'the students and the alumni to give some good, ringing cheers' to encourage the team.

Schedule

Beverly	6	Lowell	0
Beverly	0	Mechanic Arts	22
Beverly	6	Elm Hill Academy	0
Beverly	28	Haverhill	0
Beverly	6	Roxbury	4
Beverly	17	Melrose	5
Beverly	11	Everett	0
Beverly	11	Gloucester	5
Beverly	22	Salem	6
Beverly	0	Waltham	34

8 - 2 - 0

1908

Coach: Beaton H. 'Beet' Squires

Front row, left to right: A. Vernon Macauley, Albert Conley, Warren W. Bulkeley.
Second row: Fred Wittenhagen, Robert J. Cooney, Captain Bill Hayden, Bill Quigley, 'Doc' Murray.
Third row: Ralph Crosby, Karl B. Hill, Fred Wallace, Jesse Stevens, Coach B. H. Squires, Fred Cann, Horace Woodberry.

Schedule

Beverly	6	Lawrence	0
Beverly	0	Boston Latin	0
Beverly	10	Dorchester	0
Beverly	0	Mechanic Arts	0
Beverly	18	St. John's	4
Beverly	41	Haverhill	0
Beverly	23	Gloucester	0
Beverly	34	St John's (Worcester)	0
Beverly	22	Holyoke House (Harvard)	0
Beverly	12	Salem	0

8 – 0 – 2

UNDEFEATED

Through the Looking Glass

Back to 1908

The former Fire Chief Frederick Wittenhagen, a stalwart member of the 1908 team, shared in a newspaper article from many years ago his experience that surrounded the *event* that was then, and is still now, the Beverly / Salem football rivalry.

To prepare for the game, they spent the week prior living in a camp at Chebacco Lake in Essex and crossed the lake twice a day by boat to hold secret practice sessions in the Grove area. They were kept on a strict diet along with the rigorous training program.

On Thanksgiving morning, they left Chebacco Lake in a special trolley car. It took more than an hour to travel through Essex Junction, along Essex Street to Beverly, and then down Cabot Street and over the bridge to the Pitman-Brown Field.

As they took the field they must have been a fearsome sight to the Salem players for they hadn't been able to shave in over a week.

They beat Salem 12-0 that day and culminated a twice tied, but otherwise un-defeated season that featured the unbelievable statistic of having only *four* points scored against them all season.

Noteworthy

- Fred Wittenhagen, right end, rose through the ranks to become the Chief Executive Officer of the Beverly Fire Department.

- Jesse Stevens, the center, became one of Cleveland's most popular band leaders and was the director of four dance bands.

- Cornelius J. Murray, quarterback, became a Beverly Farms dentist and was the State Representative for more than ten years.

- A. Vernon Macauley, right halfback, was a famous aviator who was killed in World War I. Post One, American Legion, is named in his memory.

- Robert J. Cooney, right guard, was also killed in action in World War I. He was the first local man to die in that war and in his memory the Cooney Athletic Field is so named.

- Beaton H. Squires, head coach, was an All-American performer at Harvard before coming to Beverly. After coaching Beverly, he went on to become a successful attorney. Another interesting note is that his initials are . . . B. H. S.

1909

Coach: B. H. 'Beet' Squires

Team Listing – Does not identify photograph

Robert Cooney, Captain, Frank Hazen, Rodney Dodge, John Murphy, Neal Murray, Vernon Macauley, Warren Bulkeley, Jeremiah Cronin, Guy Stanley, Winthrop Webber, Russell Cadigan, Francis Gilbert.

Schedule

Beverly	0	Lawrence	6
Beverly	21	Holyoke H'se (Harvard)	0
Beverly	6	St John's	6
Beverly	11	Roxbury	5
Beverly	11	Hyde Park	0
Beverly	5	Haverhill	0
Beverly	0	Brockton	6
Beverly	16	Mechanical Arts (Boston)	0
Beverly	8	St Lawrence (Groton)	17
Beverly	6	Boston Latin	6
Beverly	6	H.S. of Commerce (Bos.)	11

5 – 4 – 2

1910

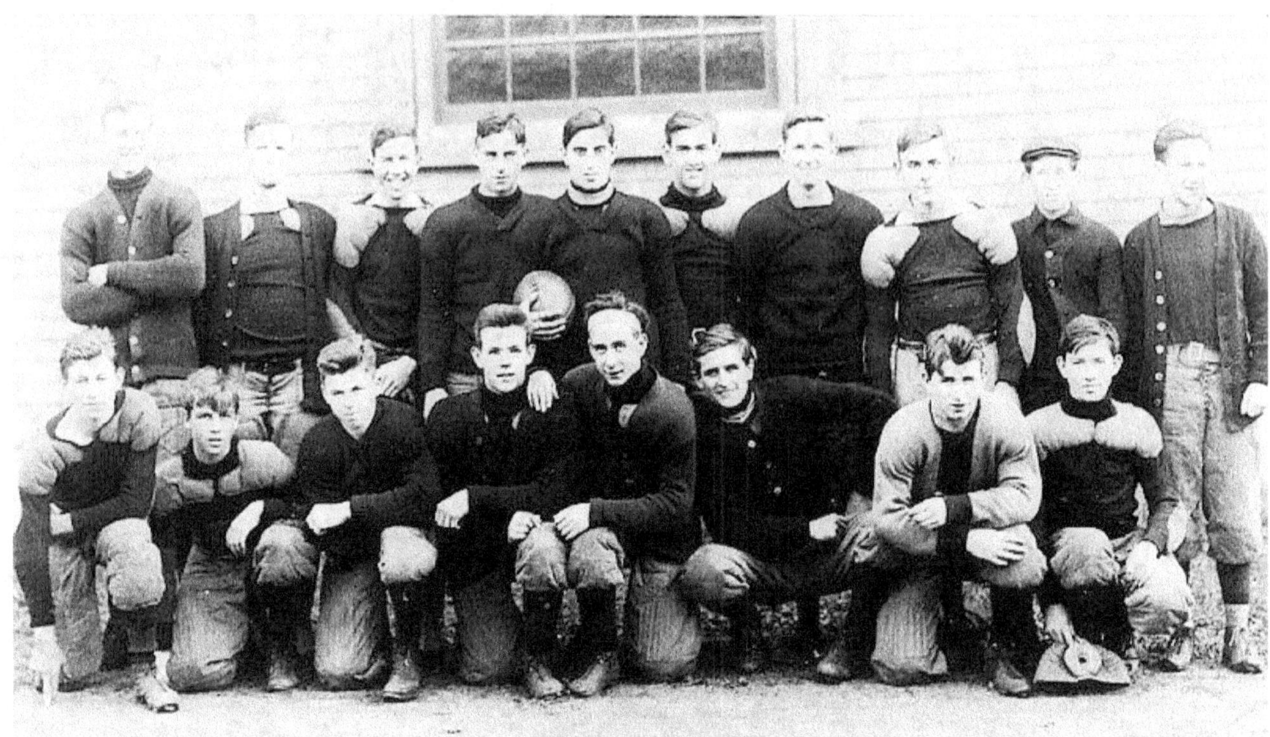

Coach: B. H. 'Beet' Squires

Team Listing – Does not identify photograph

Briggs, A. Connolly, Danforth, Davis, Stone, Mason, Pierce, Cadigan, Hunt, Murphy, Ward, Barrett, Quigley, Spencer, T. Connolly, Hillery, Lemay, Wallace, Fitzgibbon, Keegan, Legro, Cole, Macauley, Zelinsky, Dennis, Desmond, Crinon, Smith.

Schedule

Beverly	16	Roxbury	0
Beverly	0	Danvers	10
Beverly	0	St John's	12
Beverly	0	Mechanical Arts (Boston)	11
Beverly	33	South Boston	0
Beverly	6	Haverhill	0
Beverly	0	Boston Latin	5
Beverly	16	Lawrence	0
Beverly	20	Chelsea	0
Beverly	11	Waltham	17
Beverly	6	Salem	0

6 – 5 – 0

1911

Coach: B. H. 'Beet' Squires

Linemen, from left : Brown, Stone, Legro, Baker, Hood, Spenser, Desmond

Backs : Pierce, Fitzgibbons, Captain Mason, Zelinsky

(Rest of the team Listing – Does not identify photograph)

Cronin, Barrett, Wilkins, Hunt, Murphy, Soothoff, Daly,
Atkins, Cobb, McComisky, Creesy, Grey, Colby.

Schedule

Beverly	29	B.H.S. Alumni	0
Beverly	0	Haverhill	0
Beverly	0	Waltham	17
Beverly	51	South Boston	0
Beverly	11	Salem Normal	6
Beverly	3	St John's	22
Beverly	12	Beverly Industrial	0
Beverly	0	Lawrence	33
Beverly	6	Boston Latin	11
Beverly	0	B.C. High	6
Beverly	12	Salem	0

5 – 5 – 1

1912

Coach: B. H. 'Beet' Squires

Team Listing – Does not identify photograph

Hood (Captain), Macauley, Hansbury, Colby, Stone, Smith, Wilkins, Wallace, Baker, Comiskey, Brady, Daley, Nelson, Spencer, Gray, Stoothoff, Fitzgibbons, Estes, Brewer, Hubbard, Stensrud, Upton, Monahan, Ellis, Woodbury, Bowden, H.Morgan, L Morgan, Roundy.

Schedule

Beverly	14	Winthrop	0
Beverly	0	Haverhill	20
Beverly	27	H. S. Commerce	7
Beverly	7	Mechanical Arts	6
Beverly	6	Rindge Tech	0
Beverly	7	St John's	6
Beverly	0	Lawrence	13
Beverly	0	Boston Latin	3
Beverly	10	B.C. High	0
Beverly	54	Salem	0

7 – 3 – 0

The Evolution of Scoring

Prior to the 1883 season, Walter Camp of Yale, considered the founder of modern football, devised a complicated system in which each type of score a team made (touchdown, goal, etc.) was combined and measured against the combination of scores of its opponent. Confusion reigned.

Camp soon introduced a new scoring system that reflected the early game's emphasis on kicking: one point for a safety, two for a touchdown, four for a goal after a touchdown, and five for a field goal.

In 1897 the value of a touchdown increased to 5 points, and the point after was lowered to one point.

In 1912, a touchdown became 6 points, a field goal 3 points, and a safety became 2 points where they remain to this day.

In 1958 a two-point non-kick conversion was added (rush or pass).

1913

Coach: Charlie Sisson

First row, from left : Southwick, Brewer, Brady, Captain Smith, O'Donnell, Woodbury

Second row, from left : Deloid, Herron, Daley, Hosley, Fossiano, Ellis, Wright

Third row, from left : Coach C. P. Sisson, Davis, Foley, Estes, Osborne, Reid, Turner

Back row, from left : Grey, Nelson, Raymond, Stensrud, McKinnon, Creed, Atkins

(Also on team – not in picture - Hood, Heaphy, Morgan, Conway)

Schedule

Beverly	13	Huntington	0
Beverly	19	Salem Normal	0
Beverly	7	Mechanical Arts	15
Beverly	0	Haverhill	28
Beverly	6	B.C. High	6
Beverly	30	Wayland	0
Beverly	0	Boston Latin	14
Beverly	8	Rindge Tech	6
Beverly	64	Hamilton	14
Beverly	0	Salem	34

5 – 4 – 1

Manager Leslie Morgan (standing left) and Coach Jack MacDonald (standing right)
Front row from left: Charles Carbery, Assistant Manager, Captain Andrew Daley, Ralph Leighton, Assistant Manager, and James Dennis.
Second row: Clarence Stensrud, John Birmingham, Howard Morgan, and Leslie Brewer.
Third row: Walter Foley, Jack Heaphy, Willard Estes, and Linton Herron.
Fourth row: Paul Nelson, Pete Ellis, Roger Coakley, and Ralph Gray.
Fifth row: Peyer Holden, William Barron, Th___ Toomey, John Toomey, and James Cronin.
Sixth row: Arthur O'Donnel, Carl Maxner, _____, Carl Joslin, Charles Osborn, Harry Stone, and Reginald McD_____.

1914

Coach, Jack MacDonald

Andrew Daley, Captain

- Jack Heaphy was only a sophomore at the time of the picture, but his many football exploits throughout his career would earn him numerous prestigious awards including his becoming Beverly's first All-American in football at Boston College.

- Pete Ellis paid the supreme sacrifice in World War I. (Ellis Square named after him)

- James Cronin became principal of Briscoe Junior High School.

- Carl Joslin was the father of the former mayor

Schedule

Beverly	46	Gloucester	0
Beverly	19	Essex Aggie	0
Beverly	14	Mechanical Arts	0
Beverly	2	Haverhill	9
Beverly	0	Classical	0
Beverly	54	Powder Point	0
Beverly	13	B. C. High	0
Beverly	7	Boston Latin	0
Beverly	0	Rindge Tech	10
Beverly	0	Lawrence	0
Beverly	12	Salem	0

7 – 2 – 2

1915

Coach: Jack MacDonald   John Toomey, Captain

Team

Captain John Toomey, Maxner, Davenport, Flynn, Newell, Rudderham, Heaphy,, T. Toomey, Birmingham, Ellis, Eike, Herron, Albee, Holden, McNeil, Martin, Hamilton, O'Donnell, West, Coakley, Dakamonavitch, Brady, Sourier, Murphy, Price, Lakeman, Ryan, Robertson, Warren.

Schedule

Beverly	27	Peabody	7
Beverly	39	Gloucester	0
Beverly	0	Boston College High	0
Beverly	34	Woburn	0
Beverly	16	Lynn English	0
Beverly	7	Haverhill	0
Beverly	33	Chelsea	0
Beverly	17	Lawrence	14
Beverly	10	Salem	0

8 – 0 – 1

UNDEFEATED

Essex County champions

Program for Post Season game

(No score available)

Front   Back

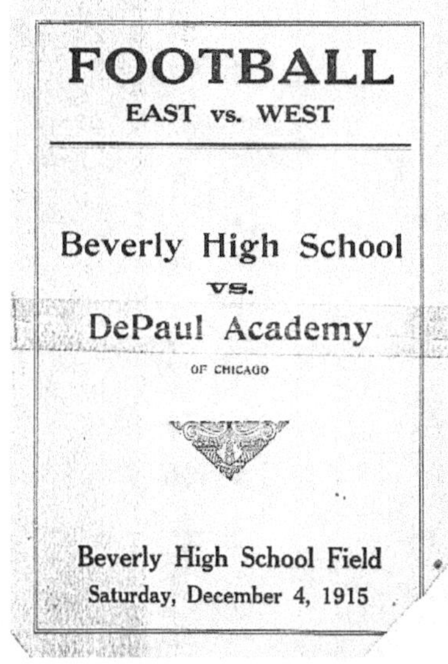

JAMES W. BRINE CO.
Athletic Supplies
Outfitters to Beverly High School
Manufacturers of
High Grade Athletic Knit Goods
Sweaters, Jerseys, Baseball, Basketball, Football and Hockey Goods. Athletic Wearing Apparel for all Sports. Wholesale Prices to Schools
1436 Massachusetts Ave.   Write for Catalog   Cambridge, Mass.

Beverly High's Statistics

Position	Name	No.	Weight	Age
L.E.	Martin	2	109	17
L.T.	J. Toomey (Capt.)	4	147	17
L.G.	Newell	6	118	17
C.	Heaphy	8	147	16
R.G.	T. Toomey	10	148	17
R.T.	Birmingham	12	148	17
R.E.	Dakamonavitz	14	123	16
Q.B.	Herron	16	140	15
L.H.	West	18	150	17
R.H.	O'Donnell	20	149	19
F.B.	Robertson	22	136	16
R.H.	Albee	24	124	16
F.B.	McDonell	26	107	16
L.T.	Eike	28	154	16
R.E.	Brady	30	124	17
R.E.	Holden	32	121	18
L.E.	Davenport	34	128	17
Q.B.	McNeil	36	115	15
Q.B.	Danforth	56	112	16

SCORE: Touchdowns

Goals from Touchdowns

Goals from Field

Safety

COMPLIMENTS OF
ALEXANDER T. MACAULEY
Candidate for Alderman from Ward Two

Central Square Lunch
BEVERLY
(Formerly Russell's)
J. P. BURKE, · Proprietor
Under New Management
THE BEST IN THE CITY
Served at Moderate Prices

WM. REED & SONS
Athletic Outfitters
BASE BALL, FOOT BALL
Basket Ball, Tennis, Track and Hocky Outfits
Sweaters, Jackets, Jerseys, Athletic Clothing, Shoes and Gymnasium Supplies
107 Washington St., - BOSTON

1916

Coach: Jack MacDonald   Captain: Jack Heaphy

1st row, 2nd from left: Jeremiah Murphy – *2nd row center:* Coach Jack MacDonald, (and next to him in sweatshirt) Captain Jack Heaphy.

Rest of the team Listing – Does not identify photograph

Roger Coakley, William Robertson, Thomas Toomey, John Newell, Arlon Albee, Everett Danforth, Jerome Flynn, Edward Ganley, William Teague, Herbert Hamilton, Philip McNeil, Arthur Landers, James Gilmartin, Gordon Rudderham, Norman Anderson, Sherman Lynch, Earle Spiller, John Davenport, Richard Gladding, Nelson Auger, John Dakamonavitch, Richard Eaton, Reginald McDonald, Earle Brotherton, Matthew Heaphy, Chester Brown, Raymond Joslyn, Foster Allen, Ambrose Robinson, Raymond McNutt, and Willis Bagley, Assistant Manager.

Schedule

Beverly	0	Quincy	18
Beverly	19	Salem Normal	0
Beverly	14	Everett	6
Beverly	0	Winthrop	10
Beverly	7	Revere	13
Beverly	0	Peabody	52
Beverly	0	Haverhill	63
Beverly	0	Lawrence	6
Beverly	10	Salem	7

3 – 6 – 0

1917

Row 2 - #1 (Angus MacLeod), Row 3 - #5 (Lewis)

Rest of the team Listing – Does not identify photograph

Coach Jack MacDonald, Captain Newell, Dakamanavitz, Robinson, Colby, Heaphy, Rudderham, Hilyard, Gray, Davenport, Lynch, Whitely, Thomas, Hubbard, Foley, Woodbury, Gladding, Boden, Fitzgibbons, Auger, Brotherton, Lucey

Schedule

Beverly	0	Gloucester	6
Beverly	23	Dummer Academy	7
Beverly	0	St John's	27
Beverly	0	Lawrence	14
Beverly	18	Essex Aggie	0
Beverly	0	Peabody	20

2 – 4 – 0

1919

Row 1 - #1 (Frank Donnelly)
Row 2 - #3 (Angus MacLeod, Captain), Row 2 - #6 (Lewis)
Row 3 - #1 (Comiskey), Row 3 - #5 (Semons),
Others: Harrington, Macaulay, Ganley, Akerley, Fitzgibbon, Dowling, Riva, Moffett, Bell, Hilyard

Schedule

Beverly	20	Watertown	6
Beverly	12	Essex Aggie	6
Beverly	2	Wakefield	3
Beverly	0	Boston English	21
Beverly	65	Lynn English	0
Beverly	0	Bentley Institute	0
Beverly	12	Peabody	0
Beverly	12	Peabody	7

5 – 2 – 1

1920

	Assistant Coaches	Captain
William McKenzie	None	James Comisky

(In alphabetical order – Not in order of seating)

Phil Couhig, Jim Comisky, Marshall Campbell, Don Davis, Doug Cameron, Vernon Cantley, John Semon, John Shay, Henry Fitzgibbons, Ted Clark, Edward Hassett, George W. (Doug) Brady, Frank Donnelly, Lester Ayers, Palmer Cressey, Dan Cronin, Joe Hilyard, Art Harrington, William Tratt.

Beverly	0	Lynn English	6
Beverly	0	Lawrence	14
Beverly	0	Ringe Tech	18
Beverly	0	Lynn Classical	32
Beverly	0	Peabody	27
Beverly	23	Essex Aggies	0
Beverly	0	Alumni	48
Beverly	0	Boston English	6
Beverly	0	Boston College High	40
Beverly	0	Salem	3

1 – 9 – 0

1921

<table>
<tr><td>Head Coach</td><td>Assistant Coaches</td><td>Captain</td></tr>
<tr><td>Elmer Fitzgibbons</td><td>None</td><td>Frank Donnelly</td></tr>
</table>

LETTER MEN

Frank Donnelly, Ted Clark, Don Davis, Phillip Couhig, Edward Pert, John Semons, Art Harrington, Rochmont Gray, Robert Smith, George Brady, Joseph Hilyard, Dan Cronin, Vernon Cantley, Lester Ayers, T. Fitzgibbons, Melnor Batchelder, William Tratt, Palmer Cressey, Callely, Durkee, John Kelley, Greeley, O'Neil.

Schedule

Beverly	36	Gloucester	0
Beverly	13	Lynn English	0
Beverly	23	Winthrop	6
Beverly	7	Watertown	0
Beverly	28	Swampscott	0
Beverly	7	Revere	0
Beverly	0	Lynn Classical	0
Beverly	7	Marblehead	13
Beverly	33	Chelsea	0
Beverly	0	Peabody	7
Beverly	13	Salem	7

8 – 2 – 1

First row, from left: #2 Ted Clark, #3 Ed Stokes, #8 George Hamor
Second row: #3 Doug Brady, #4 Coach Elmer Fitzgibbons
Names not identified: Dan Cronin, Leo Cronin, Art Harrington

1922

Head Coach	Assistant Coaches	Captain
Elmer Fitzgibbons	None	Arthur Harrington

LETTER MEN

Arthur Harrington, Robert Davenport, Doug Brady, Ted Clark, William Tratt, Ed Pert, George Hamor, Norman Hoogerziel, John Garvey, Robert Lee, Dan Cronin, Leo Cronin, Robert Smith, Paul Fitzgibbons, Palmer Cressy, Vernon Cantley, George Herron, Morton Kelley, Kieth Shangrew, John Connors, Robert Jordon, Warren Hall, Mahlon MacDonald, John Robertson, Jim McCarthy, Fred Tynan, John Sullivan, Seth Friend, Edward Stokes, William Dawson, Herman McNutt, Harry Sears, Martin Lawler, Wilber Tahoney, Dwight Hanners, Leslie Josephs, Meyer Garfinkle, Raymond Osborne, Arthur Pariseau.

Schedule

Beverly	41	Gloucester	0
Beverly	0	Winthrop	7
Beverly	0	Revere	7
Beverly	0	St. John's Prep	20
Beverly	7	Marblehead	13
Beverly	0	Lynn Classical	26
Beverly	38	Swampscott	0
Beverly	38	Chelsea	0
Beverly	0	Peabody	18
Beverly	7	Lynn English	10
Beverly	24	Salem	9

4 – 7 – 0

1923

Coach Elmer Fitzgibbons

Captain Edwin Pert

Bob Jordan

Brick Cressey

Duke MacDonald

Edward 'Fat' Stokes

Jack Entwistle

George Herron

Johnny George

Leo 'Kid' Cronin

Marty Lawler

Post Johnson

Red Porter

Warren Hall

1923

Head Coach	Assistant Coaches	Captain
Elmer Fitzgibbons	James Comisky	Ed Pert

LETTER MEN

(Does not identify photo)

Palmer Cressy, Martin Lawler, John Kennedy, Robert Jordon, Raymond O'Neil, Alfio Bertollini, John George, Mahlon MacDonald, John Entwistle, Olin Porter, George Herron, Frank Johnson, Edward Stokes, Warren Hall, Edwin Pert, Leo Cronin, Wilbur Tahoney, Raymond Osborne, Mgr.

Schedule

Beverly	0	Marblehead	0
Beverly	25	Revere	0
Beverly	6	Peabody	6
Beverly	3	St. John's Prep	55
Beverly	19	Swampscott	0
Beverly	26	Chelsea	0
Beverly	10	Lynn English	18
Beverly	6	Lynn Classical	25
Beverly	48	Gloucester	0
Beverly	0	Salem	7

4 – 4 – 2

NOTE: First Salem victory on Beverly field.

Backfield (Left to Right) – John Entwistle, Richard Jeffrey, Alex Dumas, Captain Olin Porter, George Gastonguay, Robert Bonner, Albert Turner.
Line (Left to Right) – Alfio Bertollini, Guy Reedy, Melvin Jeffs, Carl Swan, Carl Johnson, Frank Johnson, George Harrington.

1924

<table>
<tr><td>Head Coach</td><td>Assistant Coach</td><td>Captain</td></tr>
<tr><td>Marty Donovan</td><td>Rochmont Gray</td><td>Olin Porter</td></tr>
</table>

Coach Marty Donovan

Captain Olin Porter

Schedule

Beverly	13	Chelsea	2
Beverly	21	Gloucester	9
Beverly	0	Marblehead	27
Beverly	0	Peabody	8
Beverly	0	Newburyport	13
Beverly	0	Swampscott	2
Beverly	7	Lynn English	20
Beverly	0	Revere	8
Beverly	0	Lynn Classical	7
Beverly	0	Winthrop	18
Beverly	0	Salem	41

2 - 9 - 0

1925

<table>
<tr><td>Head Coach</td><td>Assistant Coaches</td><td>Captain</td></tr>
<tr><td>Marty Donovan</td><td>F. Hennessey</td><td>Melvin Jeffs</td></tr>
</table>

Linemen, left to right : Joseph Murphy, Louis Hubbard, Antonio Consolazio, William Henderson, Alex Dumas, Captain Melvin Jeffs, Robert Bonner

Backs, left to right : Clarence Auger, Wendall Murphy, Earl Swan, Brad Lamson, Walter Hubbard

(Also on team – not pictured)

Sam Hansbury, Carl Johnson, Edwin Kelley, Leo Lebel, Clarence Miller, Albert Turner, James George, Louis Woodbury, Thorndike Kent (Died – Special Award), Henry Jacobson, Mgr.

Schedule

Beverly	0	Lynn Classical	0
Beverly	0	Peabody	25
Beverly	7	Newburyport	2
Beverly	7	Gloucester	6
Beverly	6	Revere	13
Beverly	6	Winthrop	10
Beverly	0	Lynn English	6
Beverly	0	Chelsea	32
Beverly	0	Salem	41

2 – 6 – 1

NOTE: First year in new high school.

1926

Head Coach	Assistant Coaches	Captain
Herbert 'Hubber' Collins	George Cotton	Albert Turner

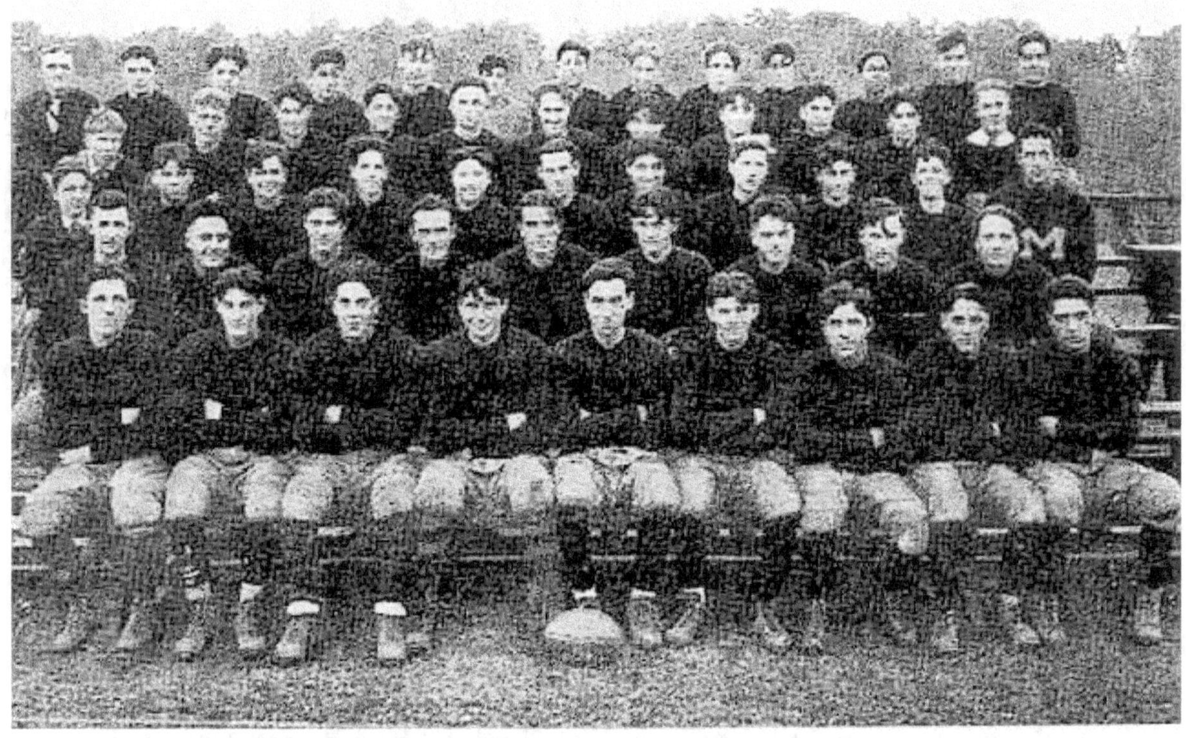

First Row, from left: Wiseman, Connolly, Waite, Couhig, Phillips, W. Murphy, Lebel, Hurley, L. Murphy.

Second Row: Burke, Consolazio, Lamson, Hansbury, CaptainTurner, Henderson, Brown, George, Seaberg.

Third Row: Morse, Hazel, Robinson, Gold, Bernson, Avery, Tosi, Ward, Pinciaro, Bromberg, Coach 'Hubber' Collins.

Fourth Row: Scott, Boyson, Tonio, Boyd, Coleman, Yeaton, McNeil, Martelli, Platon, Flannigan, Jacobson.

Top Row: Stanley, Lizio, Anconi, Nelson, Morris, Vitale, DiRubio, Buckley, Ball, Golding, Jones, Lang, Joslin.

Schedule

Beverly	6	Lynn Classical	0
Beverly	7	Swampscott	13
Beverly	6	Danvers	0
Beverly	14	Peabody	34
Beverly	16	Newburyport	6
Beverly	7	Lynn English	8
Beverly	6	Revere	19
Beverly	21	Winthrop	0
Beverly	0	Marblehead	0
Beverly	19	Chelsea	0
Beverly	6	Salem	12

5 – 5 – 1

First row from left: Baldwin, Robbins, Mgr., Couhig, Consolazio, Larivee, Hazel, Gold, Robertson, Cressy, Coach Collins.
Second row: George, Cicchetti, Nelson, Holland, LeBel, Aucone, McNeil, Lewis, Hamilton.
Top row: Steele, Lefavour, Golding, Ackerley, Chute, Flanagan, Henderson, N. Cressy, Ball.

1927

Head Coach	Assistant Coaches	Captain
Herbert 'Hubber' Collins	George Cotton	William Henderson

Jimmie Connolly

Captain William Henderson

Sam Hansbury

LETTER MEN

William Henderson, William Brown, Leo Murphy, Phillip Couhig, Antonio Consolazio, Sam Pinciaro, Leo Lebel, Sam Hansbury, John DiRubio, George Hazel, Edward Flanagan, Robert Wiseman, Flavio Tosi, James Connolly, Ralph Ward, Wesley Lewis, Don McNeil, Clement Baxter, Mgr.

Schedule

Beverly	0	Nashua, NH	27
Beverly	0	Lynn Classical	51
Beverly	16	Swampscott	0
Beverly	20	Danvers	6
Beverly	12	Peabody	6
Beverly	?	Govenor Dummer	?
Beverly	12	Lynn English	31
Beverly	0	Newton	12
Beverly	20	Gloucester	6
Beverly	6	Marblehead	7
Beverly	0	Salem	18

4 – 6 – 0

Front row from left: Ern Hinkley, Tim Holland, George Hazel, Flavio Tosi, Captain Leo LeBel, Ed Flanagan, Stu Mayberry, Ernie Henderson, Tony Consolazio.
Second row: Wes Lewis, Roland Golding, Maurice Bernson, Harry Bromberg, Bill Lawler, John DiRubio, Dick Steele, Al Aho, Art Cicchetti, Guido Aucone.
Third row: Sam Pinciaro, Stub Robinson, Jack Hurley, Dick George, Chub Poirier, Flash Cressey, Joe Maloof, Ralph Ward, Alexander McDonald, Dave Couhig, George Stevens, John Hamilton.
Back row: Assitant Coach Rullin, Earle Robbins, M. Paglia, Joe Buckley, Elmer Smith, Pinky Hamilton, Graham Nelson, Adam Ricci, Red Martin, John Cole, Curly Lentz, Bob Whidden, Coach Steve Patten.

1928

Head Coach	Assistant Coaches	Captain
Steve Patten	George Cotton	Leo Lebel

Captain Leo LeBel

Flavio Tosi

George Hazel

Harold Holland

Stuart Mayberry

Tony Consolazio

Wesley Lewis

LETTER MEN

Alfred Aho, Guido Aucone, Morris Bernson, Bertram Chute, Tony Consolazio, John DiRubio, Edward Flanagan, Roland Golding, George Hazel, Ernest Henderson, Ernest Hinkley, Harold Holland, Leo Lebel, Wesley Lewis, Stuart Mayberry, Sam Pinciaro, Norman Robertson, Flavio Tosi, Earl Robbins, Mgr.

Schedule

Beverly	0	Nashua, NH	14
Beverly	0	Swampscott	0
Beverly	33	Danvers	6
Beverly	7	Peabody	0
Beverly	6	Newton	7
Beverly	0	Lynn Classical	46
Beverly	6	Marblehead	13
Beverly	0	Lynn English	14
Beverly	7	Gloucester	6
Beverly	0	Salem	12

3 – 6 – 1

Chester Derino of Beverly contributed this photograph

Front row, from left: Dick Steele, George Stevens, Al Cichetti, Johnny George, Tony Roberto, Ira Gershaw, and Nicky DiMala.
Back row, from left: Al Aho, Dave Couhig, John DiRubio, William Thomas, and Timmy Holland.

1929

<table>
<tr><td>Head Coach</td><td>Assistant Coaches</td><td>Captain</td></tr>
<tr><td>Steve Patten</td><td>George Cotton</td><td>John DiRubio</td></tr>
</table>

Captain Johnny DiRubio

Dave Couhig	Dick Steele	Guido Aucone	Johnny George	Nick DiMala

Schedule

Beverly	6	Gloucester	13
Beverly	0	Amesbury	0
Beverly	37	Danvers	0
Beverly	13	Peabody	6
Beverly	32	Swampscott	0
Beverly	20	Lynn Classical	0
Beverly	13	Marblehead	0
Beverly	0	Lynn English	19
Beverly	19	Quincy	6
Beverly	0	Salem	13

6 – 3 – 1

(In alphabetical order – Not in order of seating)

Jack Boyson, William Bresnahan, Arthur Cicchetti, Herbert Clark, Nick DiMala, Thomas Fitzpatrick, Ira Gershaw, Francis Hamilton, Albert Harrington, John Hurley, Henry Latorella, Henry Mackey, Renaldo Mercaldi, Heath Morse, Arthur Norbaka, Charlie Pelonzi, Tony Roberto, Ted Siphol, Harold Silver, George Stevens.

1930

George Cotton

Ralph Langdell

Captain

Arthur Cicchetti

Captain Arthur Cicchetti

Coach Steven J. Patten

Henry Latorella

LETTER MEN

Jack Boyson, William Bresnahan, Arthur Cicchetti, Herbert Clark, Nick Dimala, Thomas Fitzpatrick, Ira Gershaw, Francis Hamilton, Albert Harrington, John Hurley, Henry Latorella, Henry Mackey, Rinaldo Mercaldi, Heath Morse, Arthur Norbaka, Charlie Pelonzi, Tony Roberto, Ted Siphol, Harold Silver, George Stevens, Robert Fuller, Mgr.

Schedule

Beverly	0	Gloucester	0
Beverly	12	Amesbury	7
Beverly	21	Danvers	0
Beverly	12	Peabody	0
Beverly	0	Swampscott	12
Beverly	0	Quincy	7
Beverly	0	Lynn English	26
Beverly	0	Marblehead	6
Beverly	0	Lynn Classical	0
Beverly	0	Salem	19

3 – 5 – 2

(In alphabetical order – Not in order of seating)

William Bresnahan, Herbert Clark, Nick DiMala, Ira Gershaw, Francis Hamilton, Albert Harrington, Renaldo Mercaldi, Rodney Morin, Charlie Pelonzi, Albert Rocci, Ted Siphol, Harold Silver, George Stevens, Glenn Talbot, Chester Wykes.

1931

<table>
<tr><td align="center"><u>Head Coach</u></td><td align="center"><u>Assistant Coaches</u></td><td align="center"><u>Captain</u></td></tr>
<tr><td align="center">J. Edward 'Bodger' Carroll</td><td align="center">George Cotton
Dick Moynihan</td><td align="center">Al Harrington</td></tr>
</table>

Captain Al Harrington

George Stevens

Bill Bresnahan

Glen Talbot

Nicky DiMala

'Pinky' Hamilton

'Putty' Mercaldi

Ted Sihpol

Schedule

Beverly	19	Danvers	0
Beverly	6	Amesbury	0
Beverly	6	Newburyport	6
Beverly	6	Peabody	0
Beverly	24	Gloucester	0
Beverly	0	Haverhill	13
Beverly	8	Lynn English	0
Beverly	36	Marblehead	0
Beverly	7	Lynn Classical	0
Beverly	0	Salem	0

7 - 1 - 2

Beverly High football team of 1932

Charlie Pelonzi, fourth from the right, front row, captained and quarterbacked the 1932 BHS football team to a 7-2-1 record, including a scoreless tie with Thanksgiving Day rival Salem. The coach was J. Edward (Bodger) Carroll, at left in the second row. Some of the recognizable players are: front row, forth from left, Dr Glen Hersey, who later played at Columbia; sixth from left, Al Consoni; eighth from left, Glen Talbot; eleventh from left, Nick Demala; and in the third row, seventh from left, is Peter Abate, who became a noted sculptor.

1932

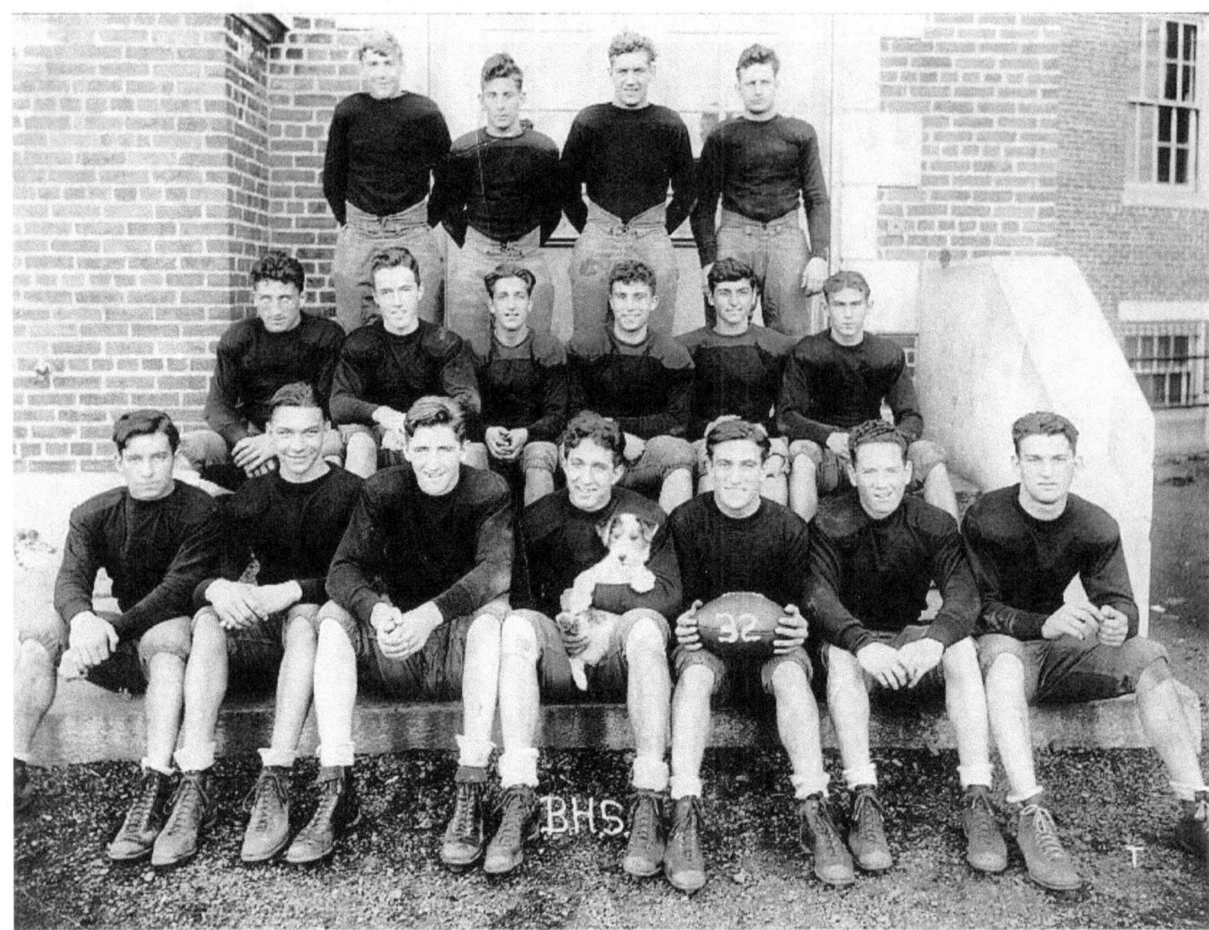

The 1932 Beverly High School football team ; (back row from left), Glenn Hersey, Harry Thibodeau, Rinaldo Mercaldi, and Bibber Lefleur ; (middle row from left), Joseph Boniface, Dan Murphy, Harry Consalazio, Vincent Defazio, Peter Abate, and Diminic Zelano ; (front row from left), Albert Rocci, Waldemar Wysocki, Glenn Talbot, Nicky Demala, Charlie Pelonzi, George Thomas, and Albert Consone.

Schedule

Beverly	0	Danvers	6
Beverly	6	Amesbury	0
Beverly	12	Newburyport	7
Beverly	13	Peabody	2
Beverly	26	Gloucester	0
Beverly	6	Haverhill	6
Beverly	7	Lynn English	12
Beverly	13	Marblehead	0
Beverly	2	Lynn Classical	0
Beverly	0	Salem	0

6 – 2 – 2

First row, from left: M. French, B. Barror, E. Santin, H. Consolazio, J. Axelrod, Captain B. Lefleur, J. Daly, R. Burns, V. Woodberry.
Second row, from left: R. Dubois, L. Howard, ________, C. Datillo, D. Murphy, V. DiFazio, G. Borsetti, B. Murphy.
Third row, from left: L. Bonaventura, D. Preston, G. Coleman, B. Malone.
Fourth row, from left: L. Bettancourt, J. Mountain, ________, ________.
Top row, from left: ________, Ass't Coach W. Wysocki, ________, Head Coach B. Carroll, D. Ginsberg, M. Latorella.

1933

Head Coach	Assistant Coaches	Captain
J. Edward 'Bodger' Carroll	Al Marsters	Lawrence 'Bibber' Lefleur
	George Cotton	

Bill Barror

Clark Shattuck

Dick Ginsberg

John Mountan

Dick Preston

LETTER MEN

Lawrence Lefleur, Peter Abate, Joseph Axelrod, William Barror, George Beaulieu, Laurence Bettencourt, Guido Borsetti, Robert Burns, Harry Consolazio, John Daley, Charles Datillo, Vincent DiFazio, Payment Dubois, Milton French, Richard Ginsberg, Lawrence Howard, Mario Latorella, John Mountan, David Murphy, Richard Preston, Ernest Santin, Clark Shattuck, Vaughan Woodbury, William Lowe, Mgr.

Schedule

Beverly	14	Danvers	0
Beverly	0	Newburyport	6
Beverly	6	Lynn Classical	18
Beverly	0	Peabody	26
Beverly	0	Melrose	13
Beverly	0	Haverhill	3
Beverly	0	Lynn English	20
Beverly	0	Marblehead	18
Beverly	6	Gloucester	0
Beverly	0	Salem	26

2 - 8 - 0

First row, from left: Joseph DiVincenzo, Ernest Santin, Charles Datillo, Captain Peter Abate, Harry Consolazio, George Beaulieu, John Malone, David Murphy, Lawrence Howard.

Second row: Hugh Nelson, Scotchie Winchester, Woodbury, Lawrence Bettencourt, Louis Bonaventura, Burnham, William Murphy, G. Coleman.

Third row: Payment Dubois, Vincent DiFazzio, Red Hansbury, Angelo Ambrefe, R. Stewart, C. Thomas, _______.

Fourth row : _______, _______, John Malloy, Harry Ball, Red Trowt.

Fifth row: _______, Ass't Coach Fish Ellis, C. Boniface, Mgr, Head Coach Bodger Carroll.

Also not identified : Anthony Silver.

1934

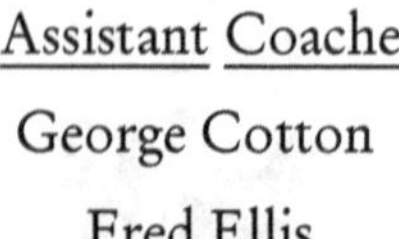

<table>
<tr><td><u>Head Coach</u></td><td><u>Assistant Coaches</u></td><td><u>Captain</u></td></tr>
<tr><td>J. Edward 'Bodger' Carroll</td><td>George Cotton
Fred Ellis</td><td>Peter Abate</td></tr>
</table>

Angelo Ambrefe

Dave Murphy

Scotchie Winchester

George Beaulieu

Harry Consolazio

Louie Bonaventura

LETTER MEN

Captain Peter Abate, Angelo Ambrefe, George Beaulieu, Lawrence Bettencourt, Louis Bonaven-tura, Harry Consolazio, Charles Datillo, Vincent DiFazio, Joseph DiVincenzo, Payment Dubois, Lawrence Howard, John Malone, John Malloy, David Murphy, William Murphy, Ernest Santin, Anthony Silver, Gordon Winchester, Charles Boniface, Mgr.

Beverly	20	Danvers	0
Beverly	6	Newburyport	0
Beverly	13	Peabody	0
Beverly	18	Melrose	12
Beverly	12	Haverhill	7
Beverly	6	Lynn English	0
Beverly	0	Marblehead	39
Beverly	13	Gloucester	0
Beverly	0	Lynn Classical	7
Beverly	0	Salem	13

7 – 3 - 0

First Row, left to right: Kenneth Frost, Harry Trowt, Walter Thomas, Brian Hansbury, Bill Cowles, John Herndon, Roger Coleman, Robert Williamson, and Freshman coach, Daley.

Second Row: Robert Brown, John Malloy, Hugh Nelson, Kenneth Frost, David Murphy, William Murphy, John Malone, Thomas Murphy, Herbert Martin, Laurence Howard.

Third Row: Frank Tanzella, Edward Holcroft, Angelo Ambrefi, Salvatore Petrosino, Laurence Bettencourt, Conte, Irving, Joseph DiVincenzo, Coach Cotton, Coach Ellis, Coach Carroll.

1935

<table>
<tr><td>Head Coach</td><td>Assistant Coaches</td><td>Captain</td></tr>
<tr><td>J. Edward 'Bodger' Carroll</td><td>George Cotton</td><td>Lawrence Bettencourt</td></tr>
<tr><td></td><td>Fred Ellis</td><td>Lawrence Howard</td></tr>
<tr><td></td><td>Freshman Coach Daley</td><td></td></tr>
</table>

Head Coach

J. Edward 'Bodger' Carroll

Assistant Coach

Fred Ellis

Assistant Coach

George Cotton

<u>NOTE:</u> This season ended the coaching career of J. Edward 'Bodger' Carroll. In nineteen years his record was 117 won, 32 lost, and 13 tied. He won 72%.

Schedule

Beverly	6	Danvers	0
Beverly	0	Newburyport	0
Beverly	40	Amesbury	0
Beverly	0	Peabody	18
Beverly	0	Lynn Classical	13
Beverly	6	Haverhill	6
Beverly	0	Lynn English	2
Beverly	0	Marblehead	16
Beverly	7	Gloucester	6
Beverly	6	Salem	25

3 – 5 – 2

First Row, left to right: W. Cowles, R. Rowell, E. Holcroft, C. Dooling, K. Noyes, R. Brown, R. Frost, F. Tanzella, J. Herndon, R. Williamson, __________, Manager J. Kelleher.
Second Row, from left: H. Martin, T. Fitzgibbon, __________, __________, __________, J. Ambrefe, R. Bromberg, __________, J. Hyland, __________.

Third Row, from left: __________, O. Scotti.
Fourth Row, from left: ?. Ellis, __________, H. Ball, __________, __________, J. Benedetti, F. Davey, Captain Hugh Nelson, R. Nadeau, __________, __________, Coach Ellsworth Richardson.

In Back, right: ?. Parkhurst

1936

Coach – Ellsworth Richardson

Manager – John J. Kelleher

John Ambrefe
Harrison Ball
John Barry
Joseph Benedetti
Robert Brown
Thomas D. Connolly
William Cowles
Francis Davey
Charles F. Dooling
Thomas Fitzgibbons
Raymond Frost
John Herndon
Edward Holcroft

Herbert Martin
Raymond Nadeau
William Nelson
Kenneth Noyes
Salvatore Petrosino
Joseph Quinn
Russell Rowell
Oscar Scotti
William Silverio
Russell Werme
Robert Williamson
Frank Tanzella

Hugh Nelson, Captain

Harrison Ball

Ken Noyes

Ray Frost

SEASON'S RECORD

Beverly	13	Danvers	0
Beverly	13	Newburyport	0
Beverly	25	Amesbury	0
Beverly	7	Peabody	6
Beverly	(Cancelled due to weather)	Lynn Classical	
Beverly	0	Haverhill	13
Beverly	6	Lynn English	0
Beverly	0	Marblehead	24
Beverly	19	Gloucester	7
Beverly	0	Salem	13

6 – 3 – 0

First row, left to right: John Holcroft, Al Montoni, Bennie Campagnola, Bill Temple, Phil Askman, Joe Quinn, Russ Werme, Joe Benedetti, John Ambrefe, Ken Noyes, Louis Paglia, Al Olszewski, Meryl Frost.

Second row: Bill Nelson, Bob Bromberg, Russ Rowell, Joe Scanlon, Barney Rantz, Al Pasquarelli, Capt. Bill Cowles, Bill Silverio, Freddy Dooling, Salvy Petrosino, Jack Barry, Jack Connolly, Ray Overberg, 'Doc' Crowley (trainer).

Third row: Bud Irving, James Pollock, Gus DiRubio, Dan Thibodeau, Doug Stantial, Frank Corning, Assistant Coach Fred 'Fish' Ellis, Coach Richardson, Dwight Waterman, Bob Tindley, Bill Moar, Allan Malloy, Charles Driscoll, William Wiseman.

Back row: Charlie Roberts, Richard Perkins, Louis Bagnell, Sam Cool, Horace Sears, Harold 'Bunk' Standley, Ted Johnson, Frank Harrington, Joe Doucette, Dan Ginty, Wentworth Murray, Paul Cheverie, Raymond McDougall.

1937

Head Coach	Assistant Coach	Captain
Ellsworth E. Richardson	Fred 'Fish' Ellis	Bill Cowles

LETTER MEN

John Ambrefe	Meryll Frost	Salvatore Petrosino
John Barry	Arthur Modugno	Joseph Quinn
Joseph Benedetti	William Nelson	Russell Rowell
Robert Bromberg	Kenneth Noyes	Joseph Scanlon
John Connolly	Raymond Overberg	William Silverio
Frank Corning	Albin Olszewski	William Temple
William Cowles	Lewis Paglia	Dwight Waterman
Charles Dooling	Alfred Pasquerelli	Russell Werme

Edward Parkhurst – *Manager*

Bill Temple   Frank Corning   John Ambrefe   Phil Askman

Schedule

Beverly	29	Danvers	0
Beverly	7	Newburyport	6
Beverly	6	Lynn English	6
Beverly	6	Peabody	6
Beverly	0	Melrose	14
Beverly	0	Medford	13
Beverly	0	Rindge Tech	13
Beverly	0	Marblehead	6
Beverly	(No game)	Gloucester	
Beverly	0	Salem	0

2 – 4 – 3

Front row, left to right: Larry McLean, Charles Roberts, Albin Olszewski, Douglas Stantial, Benny Campagnola, Barney Rantz, Arthur Modugno, Paul Fiore, Captain Joe Benedetti, William LeClerc, Gus DiRubio, Alfred Pasquarelli, John Holcroft, William Wiseman, Phillip Askman, Jack Harrington.

Second row: Coach Ellsworth E. Richardson, Thomas Stott, Allan Malloy, Pat DiCicco, Philip Beaulieu, Leonard Couhig, John McDonald, William Moar, Raymond Overberg, John Petrola, Joseph Quinn, Robert Tindley, Allan Kaplan, Nicky Petronzio, Aldo Vandi, Wentworth Murray, Manager George Thompson and Assistant Coach Charles Pelonzi.

Back row: James Pollock, Frank Harrington, Robert Dooling, Chauncey Gagnon, Paul Kessaris, Fred Robinson, Arthur St. Pierre, Daniel Ginty, Roland Jacques, Philip Arsenault, Harris Toll, Joe D'Ettore, Frank Cronin, Lyman Trask, George Barry, Terrence O'Callahan, Paul Ring, Lauri Sormunen, and John Shea.

1938

<table>
<tr><td>Head <u>Coach</u></td><td>Assistant <u>Coach</u></td><td><u>Captain</u></td></tr>
<tr><td>Ellsworth E. Richardson</td><td>Charlie Pelonzi</td><td>Captain, Joe Benedetti</td></tr>
</table>

Head Coach Ellsworth Richardson

Assistant Coach Charlie Pelonzi

LETTER MEN

Captain, Joe Benedetti	Allan Kaplan	Nick Petronzio
Philip Askman	William LeClerc	John Petrola
Bennie Campagnolo	Allan Malloy	Joseph Quinn
Pat DiCicco	William Moar	Barney Rantz
Gus DiRubio	Arthur Modugno	Charles Roberts
Paul Fiore	Wentworth Murray	Douglas Stantial
Meryll Frost	Albin Olszewski	Robert Tindley
Jack Harrington	Raymond Overberg	William Wiseman
John Holcroft	Fred Pasquarelli	George Thompson, *Mgr*

Schedule

Beverly	7	Danvers	0
Beverly	12	Newburyport	13
Beverly	6	Lynn English	0
Beverly	3	Peabody	20
Beverly	7	Melrose	7
Beverly	6	Gloucester	20
Beverly	7	Medford	0
Beverly	6	Rindge Tech	6
Beverly	6	Marblehead	13
Beverly	6	Salem	6

3 – 4 – 3

1939

Bill Foley, Head Coach

Manager
William Minigan

Assistant Manager
Richard Southwick

Assistant Coach
Dave Couhig

LETTER MEN

Philip Arsenault, Louis Beaulieu, Francis Bettencourt, Leonard Couhig, Joseph D'Ettore, Henry Dix, Robert Dooling, Frank Filtranti, Paul Kessaris, Austin Lydon, John McDonald, James Pollock, Fred Robertson, Laurie Sormunen, Thomas Stott, Arthur St. Pierre, Harris Toll, John Trowt, Aldo Vandi, David Werme, Pat DiCicco, Allan Kaplan, Nicky Petronzio, John Petrola.

Also

Richard Benirowski, Norman Peterson, Lawrence Arno, Frank Harrington, Laurence McLean, Gordon Miller.

Schedule

Beverly	0	Danvers	7
Beverly	12	Newburyport	0
Beverly	0	Lynn English	12
Beverly	0	Amesbury	6
Beverly	0	Gloucester	9
Beverly	0	Peabody	14
Beverly	0	Lawrence	6
Beverly	21	Marblehead	6
Beverly	0	Quincy	13
Beverly	0	Salem	29

2 – 8 – 0

First row, left to right: C. Story, L. Nardella, P. Ambrefe, C. Pickering.

Second row, left to right: J. D'Ettore, L. McLean, H. Toll, L. Beaulieu, P. Arsenault, A. Vandi, J. Dubois, T. Stott, F. Robertson, G. Miller, E. Gamble.

Back row, left to right: Head Coach Nick Morris, Manager Macaulay, D. Werne, H. Sciamanna, ?. Montoni, P. Mercaldi, Ass't Coach John Carr.

1940

<table>
<tr><td>Head Coach</td><td>Assistant Coach</td></tr>
<tr><td>Nick Morris</td><td>John Carr</td></tr>
</table>

The cursed curse was over. The wicked witch of Salem was dead and the yellow brick road led over the bridge to Beverly. What made it even sweeter was the victory was stirred up in the Witches own cauldron and it wasn't water that did her in . . . it was the toe of Chick Beaulieu.

'Chick' Beaulieu practicing with Aldo Vandi for
the field goal that beat Salem

Schedule

Beverly	6	Danvers	0
Beverly	6	Newburyport	0
Beverly	0	Lynn English	0
Beverly	0	Peabody	7
Beverly	7	Amesbury	6
Beverly	12	Gloucester	26
Beverly	12	Quincy	21
Beverly	7	Marblehead	26
Beverly	3	Salem	0

4 – 4 – 1

Back Row, Left to Right – Manager Macaulay, Asst. Manager LeBarron, Abbondanza, Elliott, Hathaway, McKenna, Tingley, Menkes, MacNamara, Harlow, Carr, Modugno, Coach Nick Morris.
Front Row, Left to Right – Miller, Gamble, Story, Kenney, Nardella, Capt. Bettencourt, Petrola, Smith, Ambrefe, Pickering, Sciamanna.

1941

Head Coach: Nick Morris

Captain: Frank Bettencourt

Schedule

Beverly	7	Danvers	6
Beverly	13	Newburyport	7
Beverly	6	Lynn English	25
Beverly	0	Peabody	7
Beverly	6	Amesbury	0
Beverly	0	Gloucester	20
Beverly (cancelled due to rainy weather) Lawrence			
Beverly	0	Marblehead	0
Beverly	0	Salem	6

3 – 4 – 1

First Row: (41) Clifton Story, (22) Guido Cuoco, (42) Theodore Naugler, (20) Henry Sciamanna, (40) Paul Ambrefe, (25) Donald Crandall, (38) Robert Smith, (23) Robert Campbell.

Middle Row: Eugene Lamontagne, *Manager,* (36) William Kelley, (28) Allen Elliot, (32) Sabino Modugno, (44) Joseph Hirschorn, (21) Philip Carr, (33) Joseph Celentano, (43) Robert Pelonzi, Charles McKenna, *Manager.*

Top Row: (26) Winston Naugler, (34) Waldo Harlow, Nicholas J. Morris, *Coach,* (37) Joseph Cuoco, (24) Martin Kelley.

1942

Head Coach	Assistant Coach	Captains
Nick Morris	John Carr	Paul Ambrefe
		Henry Sciamanna

LETTER MEN

Paul Ambrefe, Robert Campbell, Philip Carr, Joseph Celentano, Donald Crandall, Guido Cuoco, Joseph Cuoco, Allen Elliott, Waldo Harlow, Paul Harrington, Robert Hathaway, Martin Kelly, Theodore Naugler, Winston Naugler, Henry Sciamanna, Robert Smith, Clifton Story.

Co-captains Henry Sciamanna and Paul Ambrefe

Schedule

Beverly	6	Danvers	0
Beverly	6	Saugus	20
Beverly	12	Lynn English	0
Beverly	13	Peabody	13
Beverly	13	Amesbury	6
Beverly	7	Gloucester	6
Beverly	6	Lawrence	7
Beverly	6	Marblehead	13
Beverly	7	Salem	0

5 – 3 – 1

First Row: Allen Elliot, Phillip Carr, Joseph MacDougal, Sabino Modugno, Austin Hilton, Jerry Murphy, William Kelley, Winston Naugler, Joseph Celentano, Douglas Nelson, Victor Modugno, Frederic Bresnahan, Robert Hathaway, Daniel Tower.

Second Row: Coach Bovrini, *Manager* Vincent Nuccio, Robert Pelonzi, Ralph Fiore, Allan Whalen, Rudy Melei, Francis Roberts, Richard Bernier, James McElroy, Robert Hoar, Douglas Cram, Rudy Menesale, John Bickerstaff, Robert Pasek, John Waldie, Thomas Leavitt, *Head Coach* Henry Tozcylowski.

Third Row: John Dooling, Lawrence Atherton, Donald Richardson, Bruce Robertson, Robert Robinson, Harold Munsey, Ralph Reed, Craig Bell, Lewis Woods, Ralph Lewis, John Sciola, Jack Murphy.

1943

<table>
<tr><td>**Coach**</td><td>**Ass't Coach**</td><td>**Student Manager**</td><td>**Faculty Manager**</td></tr>
<tr><td>Henry Toczlowski</td><td>Charlie Pelonzi</td><td>Vincent Nuccio</td><td>Otis Riggs</td></tr>
</table>

From left: Bob Hathaway, Fred Bresnahan, Jerry Murphy and Sam Modugno

NOTE: No Captains were elected. The coach chose a different senior each week.

Schedule

Beverly	12	Danvers	0
Beverly	0	Saugus	20
Beverly	6	Lynn English	6
Beverly	6	Peabody	13
Beverly	6	Amesbury	20
Beverly	0	Gloucester	20
Beverly	13	Lawrence	13
Beverly	0	Marblehead	19
Beverly	0	Somerville	30
Beverly	0	Salem	13

1 – 7 – 2

Front row, left to right:
  Frank Estey, Donald Richardson, John Hilton, Domenic Petrosino, John Pietrini, John Waldie, Robert Pelonzi, *captain*, John Dooling, Ralph Lewis, Frank Marchelli, Vincent Menesale, Robert Hoar, Ernest Tedford.

Second row:
  Mr. Walsh, *coach*, Vincent Nuccio, *manager*, Stephen Femino, Francis Roberts, Joseph MacDougall, Robert Robinson, James Comiskey, Robert Diebner, Louis Woods, John Murphy, Harry Minott, Paul Desmond, Louis Mazzaglia, Charles Pelonzi, *assistant coach*, David Couhig, *assistant coach.*

Third row:
  Louis DiCarlo, Oscar Gustafson, John Carr, Dwight Hanson, Richard Tracey, Albert Romani, Guy Rossi, John McCleary, George Rogers, Richard Merritt, Carl Whitaker, Donald Cyr, Leon Mercer.

1944

Coach Dave Couhig, Coach Charlie Pelonzi, Captain Bob Pelonzi, Manager Vincent Nuccio and Head Coach Charlie Walsh

Frank Marchelli, Ralph Lewis, Jack Dooling, Robby Robinson

Schedule

Beverly	26	Danvers	0
Beverly	0	Saugus	31
Beverly	13	Lynn English	23
Beverly	0	Peabody	27
Beverly	12	Amesbury	6
Beverly	0	Gloucester	0
Beverly	12	Lawrence	7
Beverly	15	Marblehead	14
Beverly	12	Salem	19

4 – 4 – 1

First row, from left to right – George Rogers, Guy Rossi, Louie Woods, 'Brother' Roberts, Oscar Gustafson, Frank Estey, James Comiskey, Charlie Houston, Gordon Estes, Joe MacDougall.
Back row, left to right – Bill Hathaway, Paul Desmond, Gordon Zwicker, Leo Buckley, Robbie Robinson, Harry Minott, Lou Mazzaglia.

1945

Top row: Co-captains Joe MacDougal, Robbie Robinson and 'Brother' Roberts
Bottom row: Coach Charlie Pelonzi, Head Coach Charlie Walsh and Coach Dave Couhig

Robinson's kicking, passing and signal calling were among the best in the state and won for him a place on the Boston Record's All-Scholastic Team. MacDougall was a standout all season on both offense and defense, and led all ends on the North Shore in scoring 26 points. MacDougall. Mazzaglia, and Colanto were chosen on the North Shore All-Stars.

Schedule

Beverly	20	Danvers	0
Beverly`	7	Saugus	6
Beverly	27	Lynn English	6
Beverly	0	Peabody	6
Beverly	12	Amesbury	7
Beverly	21	Gloucester	0
Beverly	26	Winthrop	6
Beverly	0	Marblehead	8
Beverly	20	Salem	0

7 – 2 - 0

Front Row, from left: Rudy Modugno, Dave King, Co-captain Bob Deibner, Frank Estey, Guy Rossi, Jim Weaver, Ray Doherty, Bill Hathaway, Bob Colanto, Jack Donavan, Steve Femino, Don Dodge, Gregg Semons (Sorry 'bout the flaw).
Standing, from left: Head Coach Charlie Walsh, Roger St. Pierre, Al Gouzie, Paul Desmond, Gordon Zwicker, George Sunderland, Luigi 'Truck' Petrosino, Ray LeClerc, Walter Hayes, Richard MacDougall, Mike Toomey, Bill DiPaolo, Georges Comiskey, Co-captain Lou Mazzaglia, Assistant Coach Charlie Pelonzi.

1946

Coach	Ass't Coach	Captain
Charles Walsh	Charles Pelonzi	Louis Mazzaglia
	Dave Couhig	Bob Deibner

Schedule

Beverly	34	Abington	0
Beverly	19	Saugus	0
Beverly	12	Lynn English	6
Beverly	20	Peabody	0
Beverly	40	Amesbury	14
Beverly	14	Gloucester	14
Beverly	35	Winthrop	7
Beverly	6	Marblehead	0
Beverly	0	Melrose	33
Beverly	6	Salem	13

7 – 2 - 1

Hugh Nelson as a Pro showing his (1936) high school talent

(1939)   Bob Dooling fumbles
against Lawrence

(1939)   Clem Theberge scores to tie Lawrence
but Referee Steve Patten (ex BHS coach) says, No!

(1942)   Harrington trying to slip away
from Alex Pydynkowski of Danvers

(1942) Henry Sciamanna being mauled by
two Lynn English players

(1943)   Interference or what !!

(1944)   Jack Dooling . . . end run

(1944)   Nice catch

(1945)   Robinson (3) end runs behind Mazzaglia (1)

(1945)   Robinson (3) watches his runner go short yardage

(1946)   Bob Deibner pleading his case

(1946)   Coach Walsh and Lou Mazzaglia plotting strategy

First row, left to right: Joseph Nuccio, Manager; Donal Jarvis, Arthur Vaccaro, Fred Walker, William DiPaolo, Luigi Petrosino, Walter Hayes, James Weaver, Gregory Semons, Richard MacDougall, Leverett Campbell, George Sunderland.

Second row, left to right: Mr. Walsh, Coach, George Downing, David Laramie, Philip Lacombe, Robert Carr, Kenneth Kessaris, Austin Woods, Donald Rogers, Richard Theriault, Norman Pfaff, Michael Toomey, Donald Woodbury, Paul Kelleher, Dominic Abate, Edward Packard, Gerald Pizzello, Raymond LeClerc, Stephen Huntington, Assistant Manager.

Third row, left to right: Donald Davidson, Donald Berry, Paul Weir, Robert Fielding, George Accomando, Antonio Maggiacomo, Raymond St. Pierre, John Stuart, William Ryan, Merton Kaplan, Frank Chamberlain, Thomas Rapisardo, Thomas Wood, Philip Hanscome.

1947

Coach	Ass't Coach	Captain
Charles Walsh	Charles Pelonzi	Bill DiPaolo
	Dave Couhig	Greg Semons

Co-captain Greg Semons   Co-captain Bill DiPaolo

Schedule

Beverly	19	Wakefield	0
Beverly	0	Saugus	7
Beverly	0	Lynn English	7
Beverly	9	Peabody	0
Beverly	26	Amesbury	0
Beverly	0	Gloucester	7
Beverly	31	Winthrop	7
Beverly	6	Marblehead	7
Beverly	14	Melrose	0
Beverly	0	Salem	7

5 – 5 - 0

First row, left to right: Paul Fraser, George Brewer, Paul Kelleher, Bob Carr, Bob Hayes, Frank Chamberlain, Paul Weir, Charles Hiltunen, Nate Winer.
Second row, left to right: Joe Ambrefe, Ray LeClerc, George Accomando, Rick Filippetta, Mike Toomey, Co-Captain; Mickey Abate, Co-Captain; Don Berry, Co-Captain; Jerry Pizzello, Norman Pfaff, Sandy Kessaris, Bill Ransom,
Third Row, left to right: Coach Charles Pelonzi, Bill Wickers, Tom Rapisarda, Fred Bucci, Wayne Raymond, Lore Frost, Dick Theriault, Austin Woods, Bill Ryan, Tony Maggiacomo, Vic Menesale, Dick Evitts, Coach Charles Walsh.

1948

Coach   Ass't Coach

Charles Walsh   Charles Pelonzi

John Bochynski

Ass't Coach Charlie Pelonzi, Co-Captain Mickey Abate, Co-Captain Mike Toomey,

Co-Captain Don Berry and Head Coach Charlie Walsh

The class of '49 was blessed with one of Beverly High's greatest teams. It was the first undefeated and untied team in the school's history.

Schedule

Beverly	21	Wakefield	0
Beverly	20	Saugus	6
Beverly	13	Lynn English	7
Beverly	40	Peabody	0
Beverly	20	Amesbury	0
Beverly	36	Gloucester	7
Beverly	44	Winthrop	0
Beverly	20	Marblehead	0
Beverly	38	Salem	0
252	9 – 0 – 0		20

UNDEFEATED – UNTIED

Beverly   6 .... (Exchange Bowl). .... Brockton   14

Front Row: Charles Walsh, (Coach), John McKenna, Richard Montoni, Paul Weir, Victor Menesale, George Accomando, Dominic Abate, Harold Ransom, Frank Chamberlain, Charles Hiltunen, Charles Pelonzi, (Assistant Coach).

Second Row: Fred Bucci, Alphonse Pelonzi, Nathaniel Winer, Wayne Raymond, Richard Carr, Richard Price, Lore Frost, Andrew Beaulieu, Richard Hazell, Joseph Ambrefe, Bruce Wilkinson.

Third Row: Dwight Campbell, William Pelley, Ronald Pasek, James White, Hilton Perry, Robert Matson, Joseph Maglio, Anthony Pietrini, Robert Hayes, Charles Scobey, Charles Manuel.

1949

Coach	Ass't Coach	Captain
Charles Walsh	Charles Pelonzi	George Accomando
	Robert Brown	Mickey Abate
		Bill Ransom

Co-captains George Accomando, Mickey Abate, and Billy Ransom

Schedule

Beverly	31	Wakefield	0
Beverly	20	Saugus	15
Beverly	0	Lynn English	0
Beverly	31	Peabody	0
Beverly	28	Nashua	0
Beverly	12	Gloucester	7
Beverly	0	Marblehead	13
Beverly	20	Revere	0
Beverly	19	Salem	26

6 – 2 – 1

Front Row: Bruce Wilkinson, Wayne Raymond, Lore Frost, Joe Maglio, Joe Ambrefe, Dick Carr, Dick Hazel, Bob MacLeod, Jim White, Bob Hayes, Don Lally.
Middle Row: Fred Bucci, Dave Roundy, Dick Cunningham, Nick Maglio, Archie Chamberlain, Tony Pietrini, Bob Mattson, Charlie Manuel, Bob King, John Jaworski.
Back Row: Coach Walsh, Ronnie Pasek, Jim Duffy, John Wallace, Ted Vartzelis, Andy Beaulieu, Dick Booth, Hilton Perry, Charles Scobey, Bill Lewis, Ass't Coach Pelonzi.

1950

<table>
<tr><td>Coach</td><td>Ass't Coach</td><td>Captain</td></tr>
<tr><td>Charles Walsh</td><td>Charles Pelonzi</td><td>Dick Carr</td></tr>
<tr><td></td><td>Angelo Nicketakis</td><td>Fred Bucci</td></tr>
</table>

Co-Captain Fred Bucci   Co-Captain Dick Carr

Schedule

Beverly	27	Wakefield	0
Beverly	6	Saugus	0
Beverly	27	Lynn English	0
Beverly	13	Peabody	7
Beverly	26	Gloucester	13
Beverly	0	Lynn Classical	7
Beverly	6	Marblehead	6
Beverly	0	Revere	13
Beverly	46	Salem	13

6 – 2 – 1

First Row: Andrew Beaulieu, Robert Byrnes, Charles Scobey, Ralph Parisella, Ronald Pasek, Robert Mattson, Hilton Perry, Richard Cunningham, James Clemeno, Charles Manuel, James Duffy.

Second Row: Nick Maglio, Thomas DiPaolo, Robert Gustafson, Anthony Pope, John Mahoney, David Roundy, John Bradley, Dean Luxton, Edward Wolniewicz, Richard Booth, Donald McComiskey, Ralph Capachetti, William Wallace, William Lewis.

Third Row: Kenneth Saunders, James Corbett, Rodney Larcom, Bill Barror, John Wallace, Gerard LeClerc, Don Pinciaro, Alfred Longval, Waldo Martin, Ted Vartzelis, Donald Tosi, Tom Kelly, Richard Mattson, Donald Wilson.

Those not pictured: Gerald Dooling, John Heaphy, Roger Morency, Anthony Pietrini, Donald Robinson, Philip Rogers, Edward Stokes, David Whitaker.

1951

Coach	Ass't Coach	Captain
Charles Walsh	Charles Pelonzi	Bob Mattson
	Angelo Nicketakis	Tony Pietrini

Co-Captain Tony Pietrini   Co-Captain Bob Mattson

Schedule

Beverly	0	Haverhill	6
Beverly	19	Lynn English	13
Beverly	20	Peabody	0
Beverly	15	Wakefield	0
Beverly	21	Gloucester	7
Beverly	19	Lynn Classical	0
Beverly	32	Marblehead	7
Beverly	34	Revere	7
Beverly	30	Salem	13

8 – 1 – 0

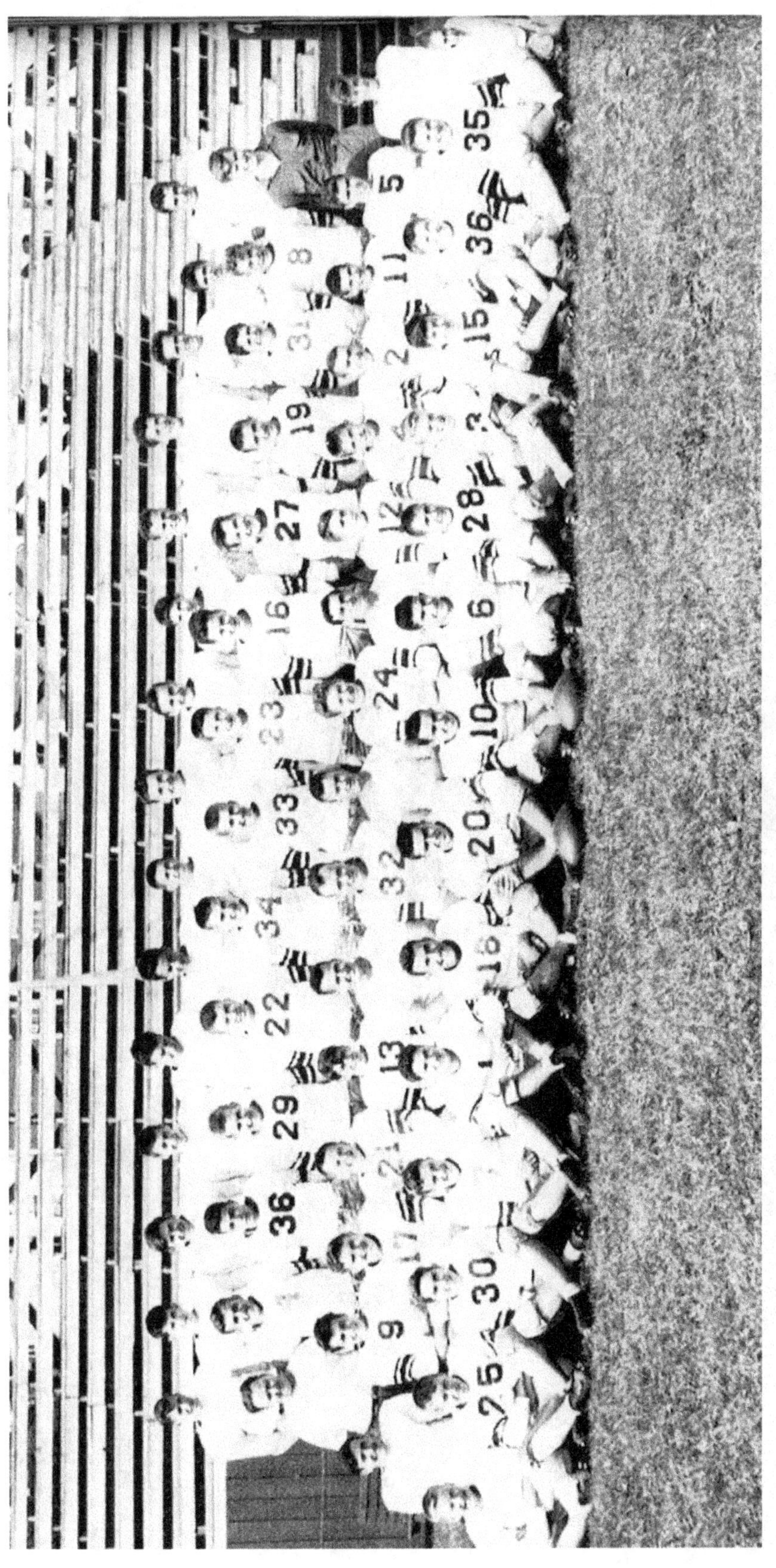

First Row, left to right: Robert Fuller, Forrest Hall, Hugh Very, William Kerwin, Nicholas Maglio, Robert Gustafson, Theodore Vartzelis, William Barror, Donald Pinciaro, Ralph Capachietti, David Bell, Alfred Longval, Robert Williams, Steven DiRubio, Donald Atwood.

Second Row: Paul Longval, Thomas Saunders, Richard Turner, Richard Matson, Frederick Carnevale, Ass't Coach John Furey, Co-Captain Dave Roundy, Coach Charles Walsh, Co-Captain William Wallace, Ass't Coach Charles Pelonzi, Roger Morency, Gerald Dooling, Gerard LeClerc, Thomas DiPaolo, William Gibbons, Lawrence Kelleher.

Third Row: Clarence Foster, Edmund Theriault, Anthony Pope, Donald Robinson, Waldo Martin, Richard Saunders, Albert Peppin, Donald Tosi, Thomas Kelly, Donald MacComiskey, John Wallace, John Mahoney, John Heaphy, Donald Hannable.

Fourth Row: Donald Wilson, Ralph Carney, Daniel Durgin, Paul McLaughlin, Robert LeBlanc, Bernard Pasquarelli, James Donahue, James Chapman, Robert Perkins, Kenneth Stokes, James Curtis, Robert LeBel, Rodney Larcom, Paul Hayes, Richard Whyte.

1952

Coach	Ass't Coach	Captain
Charles Walsh	Charles Pelonzi	Dave Roundy
	John Furey	William Wallace

Co-Capt. David Roundy　　　Coach Walsh　　　Co-Capt. William Wallace

Schedule

Beverly	7	Haverhill	21
Beverly	7	Lynn English	32
Beverly	0	Peabody	13
Beverly	0	Wakefield	14
Beverly	14	Gloucester	0
Beverly	31	Lynn Classical	0
Beverly	12	Marblehead	6
Beverly	39	Revere	0
Beverly	13	Salem	0

5 – 4 – 0

Front Row: D. Murphy, L. Tillson, J. Lawler, G. Morse, A. Consoli, Frank Bell, L. Andrews, E. Wallace, H. Ball, G. Wilder, D. Tosi, P. Guinivan, W. Gobeille, A. Manuel, J. Corriveau, W. Lund, W. Foster, P. Edwards.
Second Row: Don Tosi, L. Kelleher, W. Martin, K. Saunders, D. Turner, D. Whyte, G. Dooling, D. Mattson, D. Pinciaro, D. Wilson, D. MacComiskey, F. Conti, D. Atwood, D. Durgin, P. MacComiskey.
Third Row: D. DePiero, R. LeBel, S. DiRubio, W. Gibbons, A. Pepin, R. LeBlanc, R. Vitale, D. Bell, J. Chapman, F. Carnevale, R. Vergari, C. Pelonzi, Ass't Coach, C. Walsh, Head Coach, R. Brown, F. Hall, W. Kirwin, H. Very, Clammy Foster, Trainor.

1953

Coach	Ass't Coach	Captain
Charles Walsh	Charles Pelonzi	Don Pinciaro
	John Furey	Gerald Dooling
		Richard Mattson

Coaches and Co-Captains

Left to right: Coach Walsh, Gerald Dooling, Richard Mattson, Donald Pinciaro, Coach Pelonzi, Coach Furey, kneeling.

Schedule

Beverly	0	Haverhill	20
Beverly	19	Lynn English	0
Beverly	32	Peabody	14
Beverly	13	Saugus	14
Beverly	25	Gloucester	21
Beverly	32	Lynn Classical	7
Beverly	40	Marblehead	14
Beverly	13	Newburyport	14
Beverly	28	Salem	0

6 – 3 – 0

Front Row: Coach Pelonzi, P. McLaughlin, R. LeBel, F. Hall, W. Gibbons, S. DiRubio, H. Verry, F. Bell, J. Chapman, A. DePiero, C. Foster, Trainor.
Back Row: Coach Furey, J. Donahue, R. Brown, D. Bell, F. Carnevale, H. Ball, R. Vitale, A. Manuel, A. Pepin, L. Andrews, Coach Walsh.

1954

Coach	Ass't Coach	Captain
Charles Walsh	Charles Pelonzi	Dave Bell
	John Furey	Bill Gibbons

Co-Captains and Coach

Co-Captain David Bell, Coach Charlie Walsh, and Co-Captain Bill Gibbons.

Schedule

Beverly	26	Haverhill	7
Beverly	21	Lynn English	7
Beverly	26	Peabody	0
Beverly	25	Saugus	0
Beverly	0	Gloucester	6
Beverly	40	Lynn Classical	0
Beverly	20	Marblehead	0
Beverly	47	Newburyport	0
Beverly	40	Salem	0

8 – 1 - 0

(1947)   Salem game – Ray Carey (11), Walter Hayes (20)

(1947)   George Sunderland against Salem

(1948)   Brockton – Ransom (11), Carr (21), Toomey (32)

Pfaff (20), Chamberlain (34)

(1948) Kessaris doing his thing against Salem

(1949)   Accomando (18) and Lore Frost (8) to finish him off

(1949) Sorry, this is as far as you go

(1950) Beverly – Saugus brawl Manuel (4)

(1950) Bucci (27) blocks for

(1951) Pig Pile – Richard Cunningham (12) and Dick Mattson (21)

(1951) Charlie Manuel (4) heading for paydirt

(1952) Struggle for balance

(1954) Dave Bell (3) blocks for Fred Carnevale

Front Row, left to right: Richard Renzi, Hollis Tozier, Tony Bonjorno, Mike Tomeo, Paul Silver, Bill Marescalchi, Henry Civitarese, Mike Buchanon, Bill Whalen, Earl Carter, Steve Tosi.

Second Row, left to right: Ed Wallace, Joe Palmer, George Morse, Paul Guinivan, Co-Captain Frank Bell, Co-Captain Harry Ball, Dave Tosi, Ken Berg, Tony Consoli.

Third Row, left to right: Dave Smercrynski, John Guinivan, Tom Risoldi, Dan Hurley, Chet Frost, Warner Lund, John Corriveau, Russ Rollins, Lou Tilson, Paul MacComiskey, Bob Gobielle, Frank 'Pie' Pietrini, Arnie Allen, Bob Woodbury, Philip 'Tippy' Eramo, Coach Charlie Walsh.

1955

Coach	Ass't Coach	Captain
Charles Walsh	Charles Pelonzi	Frank Bell
	Joseph Coffey	Harry Ball

Co-Captain Frank Bell

Co-Captain Harry Ball

The Beverly High eleven ploughed through another victorious season, finishing the year with a 5-1-1 record. Coach Walsh deserves unlimited credit for turning out these battlers of 1955. For the second successive year, the Golden Warriors, with Frank Bell and Harry Ball as co-captains, captured the prized North Shore Championship. A swift decisive offense, coupled with a study defense, crumpled the opposition. Later, Harry Ball was awarded a Thom McAn trophy for his outstanding play.

Schedule

Beverly	7	Haverhill	7
Beverly	28	Lynn English	6
Beverly	27	Peabody	7
Beverly	Cancelled	Saugus	
Beverly	6	Gloucester	7
Beverly	32	Lynn Classical	7
Beverly	26	Marblehead	12
Beverly	Cancelled	Nashua	
Beverly	39	Salem	0

5 – 1 – 1

Front Row, left to right: Steve Tosi, Tom Risoldi, Phil Bright, Jim Fitzgerald, Phil Eramo, Dan Hurley, John Guinivan, Arnold Allen, Bob Woodbury.
Second Row, left to right: Richard Renzi, Jim Gibbons, Joe Starks, Tony DiVincenzo, Joe Hutchinson, Peter Dinato, John Ryan, Jack Reever, Andy Steele, Kieth Chapman, Frank Pietrini, Coach Charles Pelonzi.
Third Row, left to right: Clammy Foster, Al Menesale, Earl Carter, Tony Bonjorno, Neal Brown, Vincent Gabrielli, Jack Mills, Al Turner, David Bachman, George Gallagher, Coach John Furcy.
Fourth Row, left to right: Coach Charlie Walsh, Mike Tomeo, Peter Connery, Peter Cicchetti, Larry McDonnell, John Hendricks, Tom Dooling, Bill Hamor, Paul Silver, Mike Buchanon, David Burke.

1956

Coach	Ass't Coach	Captain
Charles Walsh	Charles Pelonzi	Daniel Hurley
	John Furey	Phil Eramo

P. Eramo, Co-Captain; C. Walsh, Coach; D. Hurly, Co-Captain

Beverly High's football team finished the season winning three games, tying one, and losing five. Beverly's wins came at the expense of Saugus, Lynn Classical and Nashua, NH, while the Golden Warriors' only deadlock resulted with Lynn English. Haverhill, Salem, Marblehead, Peabody, and Gloucester were teams victorious against Beverly. "Tippy" Eramo and Danny Hurly, two linemen who were selected to play in the Harry Agganis Memorial All-Star Game, served as the team's Co-Captains. Coach Walsh had much praise for his boys despite the team's unimpressive record.

Schedule

Beverly	13	Haverhill	27
Beverly	13	Lynn English	13
Beverly	7	Peabody	12
Beverly	20	Saugus	19
Beverly	6	Gloucester	26
Beverly	19	Lynn Classical	0
Beverly	13	Marblehead	14
Beverly	7	Nashua	0
Beverly	6	Salem	7

3 – 5 – 1

Front Row, left to right: Jim Gibbons, William Pietrini, Dave Tower, Don Aucone, Dick Hajdys, Bill Nisbet, Alan Kaplan, Paul Rhuda, Bill Lemire, Bob Fabri, Joe Maggiacomo, Peter Cicchetti, Jim Jeffery.

Second Row, left to right: Clammy Foster, Tony DiVincenzo, Joe Hutchinson, Fred Gabriel, Leo Allen, Tom Dooling, Mike Tomeo, Gordon Reid. Charlie Cunningham, Keith Chapman, Bill Hamor, Jack Reever, George Gallagher, John Ryan, Coach Charlie Pelonzi.

Third Row, left to right: Coach Charlie Walsh, Pete Connery, Larry McDonnell, Bill Marescalchi, Paul Grant, Al Menesale, Harry Civitarese, Paul Silver, Tony Bonjarno, Earl Carter, Mike Buchanan, Neal Brown, Coach Bob O'Neil.

1957

Coach	Ass't Coach	Captain
Charles Walsh	Charles Pelonzi	Earl Carter
	Robert O'Neill	

Captain Earl Carter

Tony Bonjorno

Tony Bonjorno and Captain Carter were named to the North Shore All-Star Squad.

Schedule

Beverly	13	Haverhill	7
Beverly	20	Lynn English	7
Beverly	35	Peabody	0
Beverly	6	Saugus	12
Beverly	19	St Mary's (Lynn)	6
Beverly	18	Lynn Classical	0
Beverly	14	Marblehead	0
Beverly	13	Watertown	12
Beverly	40	Salem	14

8 - 1 - 0

Front Row, left to right: Bill Lemire, Don Aucone, Keith Chapman, Gerry Pelonzi, Dick Hajdys, Paul Rhuda, Joe Starks, Bob Fabri.

Second Row, left to right: Jeff Forbes, Coach Charlie Pelonzi, Mike Tomeo, Leo Allen, Larry McDonnell, Jack Reever, Bill Nisbet, Fred Gabriel, Alan Kaplan, David Tower, Len McCarthy, John Ryan, Coach Charlie Walsh.

Third Row, left to right: Peter Connery, Paul Geary, Jimmy Gibbons, Tony DiVincenzo, Jackie Mitchell, Peter Cicchetti, Joe Hutchinson, Gordon Reid, George Gallagher, Tom Dooling, Bill Hamor.

1958

Coach	Ass't Coach	Captain
Charles Walsh	Charles Pelonzi	John Ryan
	Robert O'Neill	Mike Tomeo
	Norman Rand	

Co-captain Mike Tomeo   Co-captain John Ryan

Coach Charlie Walsh

SEASON'S RECORD

Beverly	6	Haverhill	6
Beverly	30	Lynn English	0
Beverly	41	Peabody	14
Beverly	34	Saugus	0
Beverly	28	Gloucester	0
Beverly	34	Lynn Classical	0
Beverly	35	Marblehead	0
Beverly	47	Watertown	8
Beverly	47	Salem	19

8 – 0 – 1

UNDEFEATED

Front Row: W. Pietrini, K. Darcy, D. Aucone, R. Hadjys, R. Gut, W. Nisbet, R. Fabri, W. Lemire, P. Rhuda, R. Morse, A. Kaplan, K. DiRubio, R. Harrington.
Second Row: D. Guinivan, N. Ciani, S. Abbott, J. Scotti, T. Smith, R. Hoar, W. Fabri, K. Liporto, T. Siihpol, P. Tosi, W. Sargent, J. Carrato, W. Normand, T. Treacy, R. Goldberg, J. Andreas, R. Russell, K. MacDonald, Mr O'Neill, Coach.
Third Row: W. Quigley, J. Carnavale, J. Forbes, N. Whittridge, A. Ryan, W. Earle, C. Moser, D. Roberts, R. Costa.

1959

Co-Captain 'Red' Fabri   Co-Captain Bill Lemire

Coach Roy Norden

SEASON'S RECORD

Beverly	12	Haverhill	6
Beverly	46	Lynn English	14
Beverly	8	Peabody	14
Beverly	6	Saugus	18
Beverly	8	Gloucester	0
Beverly	44	Lynn Classical	0
Beverly	20	Marblehead	6
Beverly	6	Watertown	14
Beverly	0	Salem	2

5 – 4 – 0

First Row: A. Menesale, T. Smith, T. Sihpol, S. Abbott, J. Andreas, R. Russell, R. Goldberg, P. Tosi, Co-Captain W. Earle, Co-Captain D. Roberts, J. Scotti, K. MacDonald, W. Sargent, N. Ciani, E. Zubriel,
Second Row: W. Fabri, R. Rogers, J. Delisio, D. Litka, R. Wallace, D. Connell, R. Frost, R. Fortunato, J. Carnevale, J. Carratu, D. Guinivan, K. Liporto, W. Porreca, K. Pelonzi.
Third Row: Head Coach Roy Norden, Coach J. Flumere, S. Harrington, W. Carr, C. Frost, J. Joyce, R. Ellis, W. Grant, M. McPherson, R. Winquist, B. Shea, A. Witwicki, D. Manuel, C. Overberg, Trainer C. Foster, Coach R. O'Neill.

1960

Co-Captain Bill Earle   Co-Captain Don Roberts
Coach Roy Norden

SEASON'S RECORD

Beverly	18	Haverhill	8
Beverly	6	Lynn English	0
Beverly	46	Peabody	6
Beverly	14	Saugus	0
Beverly	30	Gloucester	0
Beverly	20	Danvers	0
Beverly	38	Newton	8
Beverly	14	Watertown	8
Beverly	8	Salem	6

9 – 0 - 0

UNDEFEATED - UNTIED

Front Row: C. Young, J. Hendrickson, D. Manuel, B. Shea, J. Joyce, R. Ellis, W. Grant, W. Carr, R. Wallace, R. Frost, C. Overberg, D. Weaver.
Second Row: S. Glover, C. Frost, M. McPherson, S. Harrington, R. Rodgers, W. Porreca, D. Connell, A. Witwicki, R. Fortunato, R. Winquist, G. Wallace, K. Pelonzi, M. Harrington.
Third Row: T. Cockfield, D. Litka, J. Delisio, D. Cucinelli, A. Brewster, W. Chin, F. Foley, W. Presson, R. Lister, P. Santamaria, R. Pinciaro, D. Smith, R. Aucone, P. Zeitzoff, T. Ballantine, C. Harrington.

1961

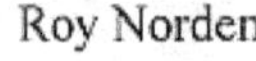

(Coaches)
John Doherty   Louis Flemire
Roy Norden

Co-Captain
Robert Ellis

Co-Captain
Walter Grant

Schedule

Beverly	12	Haverhill	0
Beverly	44	Saugus	0
Beverly	32	Peabody	0
Beverly	8	Lawrence	12
Beverly	38	Gloucester	0
Beverly	30	Danvers	6
Beverly	44	Newton	22
Beverly	12	Brookline	6
Beverly	48	Salem	0

8 – 1 – 0

First Row: B. Fumerola, R. Young, P. Zeitzoff, F. Foley, T. Cockfield, D. Smith, D. Manuel, C. Overberg, D. Weaver, W. Presson, J. Hendrickson, R. Pinciaro.
Second Row: A. Harrington, W. Chin, A. Brewster, R. Aucone, P. Santanaria, B. Silverio, D. Cucinelli, J. Sihpol, D. Vitale, J. Lewis, R. Coletti.
Third Row: Roy Norden (Head Coach), George Accomando (Back Coach), L. Foan, T. Ballantine, T. Lemire, P. Predka, R. Beaulieu, D. McKenna, T. Ervin, T. Gallagher, B. Butterworth, M. Ryan, W. Cottle, D. Wilkins, M. Coughlin, B. Dockham, K. Overberg, John Doherty (Line Coach), C. Foster (Trainer).

1962

Co-Captains

Dave 'Bippy' Manuel   Danny Smith

SEASON'S RECORD

Beverly	38	Haverhill	0
Beverly	42	Saugus	0
Beverly	28	Peabody	6
Beverly	28	Lawrence	20
Beverly	20	Gloucester	18
Beverly	22	Danvers	6
Beverly	30	Newton	16
Beverly	20	Brookline	22
Beverly	46	Salem	0

8 – 1 – 0

Bottom Row: D. Wilkins, W. Coletti, M. Ryan, T. Erwin, J. Sihpol, T. Gallagher, K. Overberg.
Second Row: J. Levine, S. Nile, R. Borsetti, G. Townshend, S. Davidson, R. Tiori.
Top Row: C. Chenard, D. Oherne, G. Miller, P. Johnson, J. Forte.

Bottom Row: M. Coughlin, T. Lemire, B. Dockham, D. McKenna, D. Vitale, G. Coteraro, R. Beaulieu.
Second Row: L. Bennett, R. Burke, B. Black, G. Smith, R. Wallace, D. Vagos, W. Cottle.
Top Row: R. Foley, B. Feldman, D. Eaton, J. Wiley, J. Aucone.

1963

Mr Kinnaly (JV Coach), Mr Accomando (Backfield Coach), Mr Lapsley (Line Coach),
Mr Norden (Head Coach), Mr Foster (Trainer), Mr Sanborn (JV Coach)

Co-Captains T. Erwin and D. McKenna

SEASON'S RECORD

Beverly	12	Haverhill	14
Beverly	28	Saugus	0
Beverly	22	Peabody	6
Beverly	22	Lawrence	8
Beverly	36	Gloucester	15
Beverly	22	Danvers	8
Beverly	0	Newton	14
Beverly	6	Brookline	38
Beverly	0	Salem	42

5 – 4 – 0

(1954)   Fred Carnevale (33) out-running Salem players

(1956)   Put me in, Coach !!

(1956)   Tony Divincenzo (22), Phil Eramo (23)

(1958)   Mike Tomeo heads for paydirt

(1958)   Tony DiVincenzo draws a crowd

(1959)   Jeff Forbes around right end

(1960) Wally Grant against Salem

(1960)   Tough yardage

(1961)   A clip clears the way !

(1962)   Not much there this time

(1962) Bippy Manuel runs to daylight

(1963)   While beating Saugus 28-0

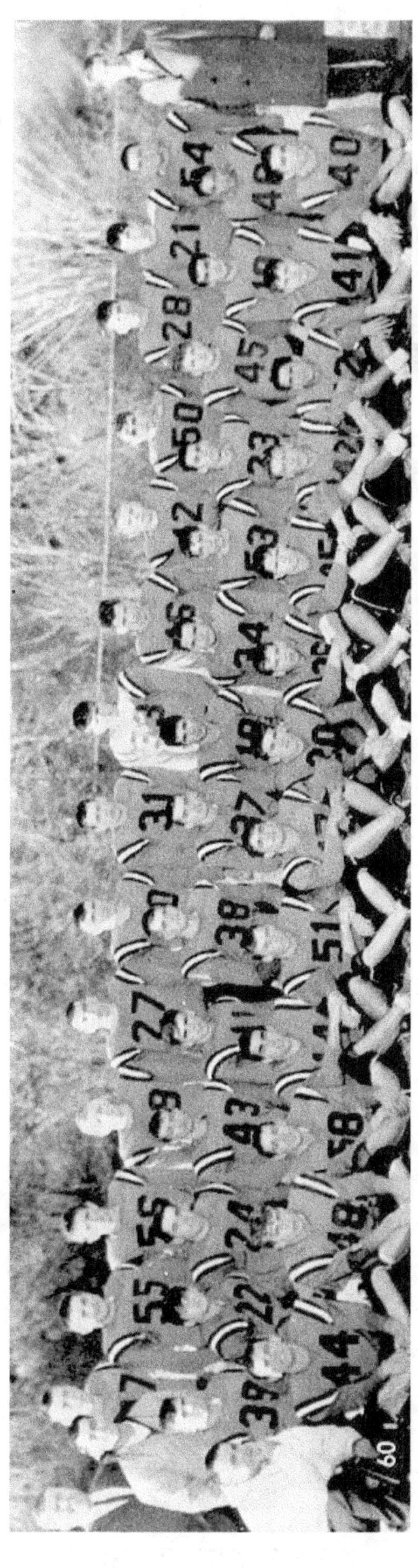

Bottom Row: Coach Accomando, R. Wallace, S. Davidson, S. Melei, B. Black, D. Eaton, P. Johnson, D. Tomeo, B. Butterworth, G. Smith, G. Nardella, C. Bixbee, J. Forti.
Middle Row: J. Vaccaro, B. Carnevale, R. Tingley, R. Fiore, G. Miller, B. Feldman, R. Foley, A. Tilas, R. Borsetti, W. Morrison, J. Levine, R. Morse, G. Copelas, C. Ellis.
Top Row: Coach Lapsley, D. Vagos, T. Bates, R. Shaw, L. Femino, J. Davey, D. Markham, T. Liporto, J. Corbett, G. Stephanos, D. Gauthier, R. Walsh, M. McPherson, P. Connaughton, P. Carr, V. Difazio, Coach Norden.

1964

Coach Lapsley Coach Norden Coach Accomando

Co-captain Bruce Butterworth

Co-captain Peter Johnson   Co-captain Dave Tomeo

SEASON'S RECORD

Beverly	16	Haverhill	12
Beverly	36	Saugus	6
Beverly	30	Peabody	12
Beverly	14	Lawrence	0
Beverly	36	Gloucester	14
Beverly	32	Danvers	6
Beverly	44	Newton	14
Beverly	26	Brookline	6
Beverly	50	Salem	12

9 - 0 - 0

UNDEFEATED - UNTIED

First Row: M. Wilson, K. Noonan, V. DiFazio, R. Walsh, D. Gauthier, M. McPherson, R. Morse, P. Carr.
Second Row: D. Dube, W. Hardenbrook, T. Bates, C. Ellis, G. Stephanos, J. Corbett, J. Vaccaro, D. Markham.
Third Row: Coach R. Norden, R. Trudeau, K. Clark, M. Crowley, P. Connaughton, R. Koen, J. Davey, G. Copelas, T. Roccio, Coach Southwick.
Fourth Row: Coach Arangio, Trainer C. Foster, S. Robins, C. Williams, R. Marino, P. Kennedy, A. Morris, P. Miller, G. Randall, Coach Kinnaly.
Top Row: D. Gray, P. Corriveau, M. McCarthy, P. Fiore, M. Carnevale, R. LaBrie, P. McFadden, H. Smith, C. Bulger, Coach Lapsley.

1965

Myles McPherson (50), Ron Morse (45) and Jim Corbett (31)
with Roy Norden (Head Coach)

SEASON'S RECORD

Beverly	18	Haverhill	0
Beverly	20	Saugus	20
Beverly	26	Peabody	32
Beverly	8	Lawrence	27
Beverly	16	Gloucester	0
Beverly	28	Danvers	0
Beverly	26	Newton	0
Beverly	12	Lowell	0
Beverly	20	Salem	6

6 – 2 - 1

Bottom Row: R. Marino, P. Miller, P. Kennedy, H. Smith, P. Corriveau, P. Fiore, P. McFadden, 'Gongas', M. Carnevale, R. LaBrie, R. Trudeau, M. Crowley, W. Hardenbrook, M. Wilson, J. Higby.
Middle Row: Coach Kinnaly, C. Bulger, J. Powers, C. Williams, P. Teague, B. Scanlon, M. Miedjionski, J. Hall, D. Lunn, K. Murphy, G. Morrison, J. MacDonald, G. Cyr, M. Cahill, M. McCarthy, C. Foster (Trainer).
Top Row: Coach Norden, J. Kelleher, D. Dube, S. Robbins, G. Randall, N. Mitchell, L. Goldberg, M. Conley, A. Norris, C. Sandy, J. Wright, G. Overberg, J. Brewer, S. Borsanti, R. Cutraro, G. Davison, J. Glasser, Coach Lapsley, Coach Arangio, Coach Southwick.

1966

Richard Southwick, John Lapsley, Roy Norden (Head Coach), George Kinnaly, Domenic Arangio.

Co-Captains: P. Miller   P. McFadden

SEASON'S RECORD

Beverly	14	Haverhill	20
Beverly	8	Saugus	36
Beverly	24	Peabody	22
Beverly	0	Lawrence	20
Beverly	6	Gloucester	6
Beverly	14	Danvers	34
Beverly	6	Notre Dame	6 *
Beverly	8	Lowell	13
Beverly	8	Salem	30

* They came from West Haven, CT and were a four touchdown favorite

1 – 6 – 2

Bottom Row: J. Hall, M. Conley, P. Teague, G. Vandi, R. Marino, A. Morris, C. Sandy, L. Hartwell, D. Lunn.
Second Row: C. Mitchell, N. Mitchell, G. Overberg, J. Powers, G. Randall, T. Larson, R. Foustoukus, J. Drinkwater, M. Hill, C. Bulger.
Third Row: H. Connaughton, S. Foss, P. Comeau, P. Barry, R. Melie, J. Frazier, B. Rhoades, J. Ricci, C. Hartnett, R. DiNicola.
Top Row: R. Catraro, J. Robinson, T. Lee, W. Charette.

1967

Co-Captains

Ronald Marino   Allen Morris

SEASON'S RECORD

Beverly	12	Haverhill	6
Beverly	30	Saugus	6
Beverly	32	Peabody	6
Beverly	22	Lawrence	8
Beverly	14	Gloucester	18
Beverly	46	Danvers	6
Beverly	38	Everett	18
Beverly	6	Lowell	33
Beverly	12	Salem	28

6 – 3 – 0

Bottom Row: J. Glasser, P. Murray, G. Davison, R. Cotraro (Co-Captain), N. Mitchell (Co-Captain), T. Lee, H. Connaughton, L. Crofts.

Second Row: C. Hartnett, J. Frazier, S. Foss, R. Foustoukus, J. Drinkwater, T. Larson, P. Barry, M. Hill, R. Melei.

Third Row: Assistant Coach John Lapsley, P. Nelson, W. Foley, J. Musumeci, G. Congley, G. Marcean, W. Charette, G. Dubois, P. Comeau, R. Melei.

Fourth Row: Head Coach Roy Norden, G. Bennett, B. Bulger, D. Smith, W. Philpot, J. Dawson, J. Hirschfeld, R. Carr, A. Carr, M. Casey, Clammy Foster (Trainer), Assistant Coach George Kinnaly.

Fifth Row: R. Allen, D. Smorczewski, J. Andreas, B. Shea, D. Ober, J. Modugno, D. Modugno, S. Collins, D. Dowling, W. St Pierre, M. Cronin.

1968

Coach	Ass't Coach	Captain
Roy Norden	Jack Lapsley	Rich Cotraro
	George Kinnaly	Neil Mitchell

Co-captains Rich Cotraro and Neil Mitchell

SEASON'S RECORD

Beverly	0	Haverhill	12
Beverly	22	Saugus	6
Beverly	8	Peabody	38
Beverly	38	Lawrence	8
Beverly	12	Gloucester	13
Beverly	6	Lynn English	8
Beverly	20	Everett	50
Beverly	36	Lowell	16
Beverly	12	Salem	0

4 – 5 – 0

First Row: D Hubbard, P. Lawler, W. Philpot, J. Hirschfeld, J. Musemeci, J. Dawson, R. Allen, D. Smith, B. Bulger, P. Quill, D. Smorczewski, P. Chalifour, J. Andreas, K. Rigby.
Middle Row: P. Polonsky, D. Pierpont, J. Modugno, W. St. Pierre, R. Zegaczewski, R. Melci, P. Moore, N. Desmond, A. Carr, R. Carr, J. Allen, T. Tarricone, P. Kelly, D. Modugno.
Top Row: P.Morris, B. Condon, V. Gaudenzi, R. Josselin, P. Bulger, D. Dowling, A. Drinkwater, D. Obear, B. Quigley, G. Congley, F. Marchelli, L. Flannery, P. Welch, B. Josselin, J. Woods, B. Shea, G. Bennett.

1969

Head Coach	Ass't Coach	Tri-Captains
Roy Norden	Bill Hamor	Ray Allen
	Jack Lapsley	Jim Dawson
	Tony Witwicki	Joel Musemeci
	Niles Flanders	

Co-captains Joel Musemeci, Jim Dawson and Ray Allen

SEASON'S RECORD

Beverly	22	Haverhill	34
Beverly	20	Saugus	28
Beverly	0	Peabody	20
Beverly	30	Lawrence	14
Beverly	16	Gloucester	20
Beverly	22	Lynn English	14
Beverly	14	Everett	6
Beverly	6	Lowell	25
Beverly	28	Salem	44

3 – 6 – 0

(1963)   Great catch against Saugus

(1964)   George Copelas begins
a punt return

(1964)   Dave Tomeo off tackle
to paydirt against Peabody

(1965)   Too much for Danvers on this day

(1965) Connaughton on a tear

(1966) Randall (14), Powers (16) against Notre Dame Academy

(1966) Bulger throws a bomb against Notre Dame Academy while
Marino (59) and Hardenbrook (58) block

(1967) Glenn Randall catching
a tough one

(1968) Congley pulls away

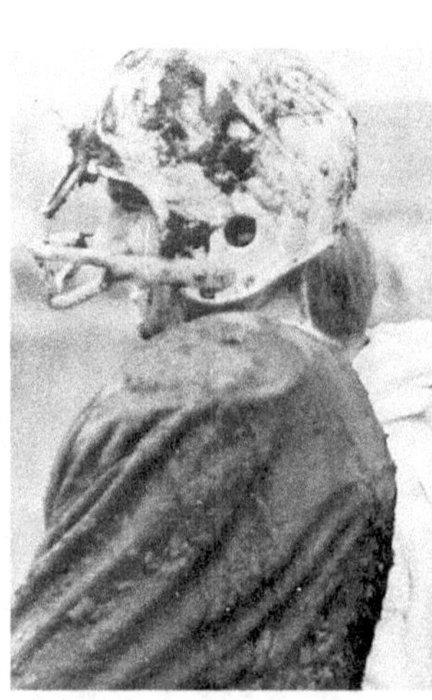

(1968) Ray Allen, triumphant, battered
warrior

(1969) Touchdown !!

(1969) Anxious moments

First Row: Coach Bill Hamor, F. Marchelli, R. Rigby, N. Desmond, D. Modugno, J. Allen, J. Modugno, D. Pierpont.
Second Row: R. Spiridigliozzi, R. Maniates, J. Roberts, T. Alexander, J. Woods, D. Ober, B. Shea.
Third Row: Coach Ed McFarland, J. Morris, P. Bulger, M. Phelan, M. Thompson, R. St. Charles, S. Shipp, J. Egan.

First Row: P. Welch, M. Collins, V. Goudenzi, W. Condon, D. Dowling, R. Josselin, P. Kelly.
Second Row: L. Flannery, A. Drinkwater, M. Thompson, M. Gongas, M. Carusi, D. Lee, D. Fall, H. Deschamps, Trainer C. Foster.
Third Row: K. Dodge, J. Nichols, F. Santin, B. Connolly, W. Bourque, J. O'Brien, J. Barry, R. Levasseur, Head Coach Roy Norden.

1970

Head Coach	**Ass't Coach**
Roy Norden	Bill Hamor
	Ed McFarland

Tri-captains – Dave Pierpont, Phil Welch, Dave Modugno

SEASON'S RECORD

Beverly	24	Haverhill	0
Beverly	6	Arlington	7
Beverly	28	Peabody	6
Beverly	14	Lawrence	15
Beverly	20	Gloucester	14
Beverly	38	Lynn English	12
Beverly	38	Everett	24
Beverly	8	Lowell	30
Beverly	30	Salem	12

6 - 3 - 0

(In alphabetical order – Not in order of seating)

T. Alexander, S. Bee, B. Brown, P. Bulger, M. Carusi, J. Celantano, M. Colanto, G. Congley, R. Connolly, H. Deschamps, D. Fall, M. Gongas, T. Harney, K. Henebury, M. Kinback, D. Lee, R. Levasseur, R. Mace, S. Mahoney, B. McDonald, R. MacNeil, D. Moran, J. Morris, J. Nichols, B. O'Beirn, J. O'Brien, M. Phalen, R. Pierce, J. Pietrini, G. Putur, B. Quigley, G. Rogers, F. Santin, R. St. Charles, S. Shupp, R. Spiridigliozzi, D. Wallace, R. Whitaker.
Head Coach Roy Norden, Assistant Coach Bill Hamor, Assistant Coach Noel Rebennacker, and M. Bussone, Manager

1971

Head Coach	Ass't Coach	Captains
Roy Norden	Bill Hamor	Mike Carusi
	Noel Reebenacker	Peter Bulger
	Roger Rosinski	Henry Deschamps
	Niles Flanders	

Coach Norden with Tri-Captains M. Carusi (just out of the picture), H. Deschamps and P. Bulger.

The 1971 Beverly High School football team enjoyed a 6–3 record and was coached by Roy Norden. He was assisted by Noel Reebenacker and Bill Hamor. The junior varsity and sophomore teams were coached by Niles Flanders, Bill Hamor and Roger Rosinski. The Thanksgiving game was memorable for the pouring rain, but the loyal fans showed up at Hurd Stadium to watch the Panthers *drown* the Salem Witches 14-8.

SEASON'S RECORD

Beverly	8	Haverhill	3
Beverly	12	Arlington	27
Beverly	14	Peabody	30
Beverly	22	Lawrence	9
Beverly	28	Gloucester	8
Beverly	18	Lynn English	14
Beverly	16	Everett	14
Beverly	0	Lowell	7
Beverly	14	Salem	8

6 – 3 - 0

First Row (Left to Right): P. Miedzionoski, M. Colanto, J. Pietrini, B. MacDonald, D. Wallace (Tri-Captain), M. Kinback (Tri-Captain), R. MacNeill (Tri-Captain), R. Rice, J. Carr.

Second Row: G. Rogers, R. Williamson, G. Smith, R. Melei, B. Brown, P. Scanlon, T. Harney, S. Barror, K. Henebury, J. Celentano, J. Rigby.

Third Row: F. Lavigne (Manager), T. Hogan, R. Frongillo, T. Porter, N. Real, J. Lawrence, S. Treantos, S. Kaylor, G. Putur, J. Lunn, M. Cronan, M. Jenness, J. Nichols, J. Kelly.

Top Row: S. Clark, P. Hayes, R. Hutchinson, P. Hutt, M. Nardella, R. Eldridge, M. Flynn, E. Hannable, A. DiPaolo, B. Nardella, J. Chludzenski, P. Morris, M. Fraser, D. Spiridigliozzi, L. Burns.

135

1972

Head Coach	Ass't Coach	Tri-Captains
Roy Norden	Bill Hamor	Don Wallace
	Noel Reebenacker	Mark Kinback
	Roger Rosinski	Bruce MacDonald
	Niles Flanders	

Tri-captains Don Wallace, Mark Kinback and Bruce MacDonald

SEASON'S RECORD

Beverly	0	Haverhill	28
Beverly	6	Arlington	12
Beverly	0	Peabody	20
Beverly	8	Lawrence	20
Beverly	14	Gloucester	14
Beverly	6	Lynn English	22
Beverly	0	Everett	24
Beverly	18	Lowell	8
Beverly	8	Salem	17

1 – 7 – 1

Bottom Row: Jr. Manager R. Pelletier, L. Burns, D. Spiridigliozzi, R. Pero, P. Hutt, N. Real, E. Hannable, J. Lawrence, B. Hutchinson, M. Jenness, J. Kelly, P. Tosi, M. Theriault, M. McPherson.

Middle Row: Soph. Manager W. Brewer, P. Miedzionoski, R. Castellucci, M. Bushey, B. Nardella, M. Fraser, R. Frongillo, J. Kleemola, D. Coletti. Tri-Captain M. Cronan, S. Treantos. J. Lunn, J. Chludzenski, P. Hayes, M. Nardella, Trainer C. Foster.

Top Row: Assistant Coach R. Rosinski, Assistant Coach W. Hamor, B. Nardella, K. Richardson, R. Carnevale, P. Smith, M. Connaughton, B. Flynn, W. Heckman, T. Richardson, M. Flynn, W. Cavley, J. Nichols, Tri-Captain G. Putur, Tri-Captain S. Kaylor, G. Dockham, R. Logan, Head Coach Roy Norden.

137

1973

Head Coach	**Ass't Coach**	**Tri-Captains**
Roy Norden	Bill Hamor	Mark Cronan
	Roger Rosinski	Gary Putur
		Steve Kaylor

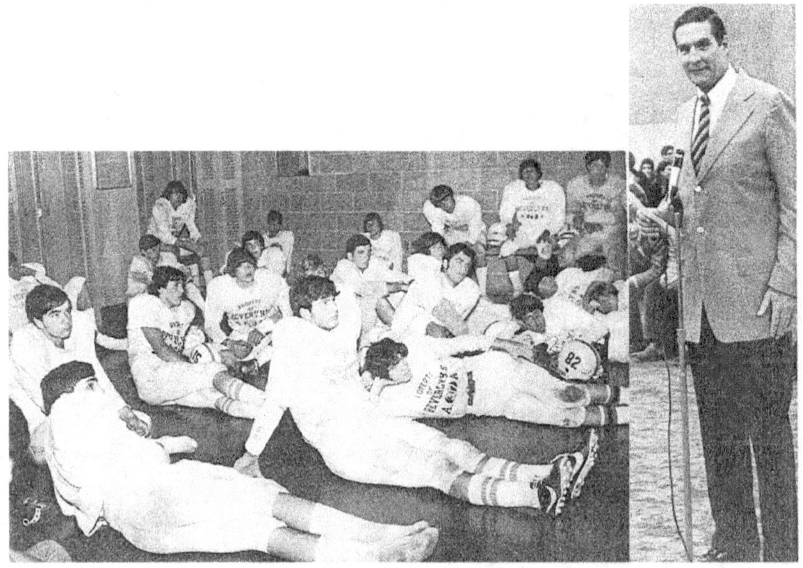

Addressing the troops

SEASON'S RECORD

Beverly	22	Haverhill	44
Beverly	36	Lynn English	14
Beverly	6	Peabody	24
Beverly	16	Lawrence	0
Beverly	14	Gloucester	6
Beverly	16	Winthrop	0
Beverly	6	Lowell	14
Beverly	6	Salem	14

4 – 4 – 0

Bottom from left: Trainer C. Foster, W. Heckman, P. Smith, B. Nardella, D. Colletti, M. Bushey, B. Flynn, W. Cauley, J. Kleemola, M. Castellucci, T. Richardson, S. Upham, D. Carnevale, G. Dockham, M. Connaughton, J. Chludenski.

Middle Row: Coach Rosinski, A. DiPaolo, D. Smith, S. LeBell, J. Zaginailoff, T. Hammond, A. Landers, M. Desmond, C. Eagan, G. Treantos, B. Nardella, B. Archibald, S. Thomas, M. McPherson, D. Musenechi, P. Coyle, Coach Hamor.

Top Row: Manager B. Brewer, E. O'Reilly, M. Theriault, A. French, S. Wallace, M. Allen, J. Grein, K. Richardson, K. Menesale, D. Ganey, M. Ventre, J. Rice, M. Ricker, J. Trembaly, J. Ambrefe, S. Hayes, Head Coach Roy Norden.

1974

Head Coach	Ass't Coach	Tri-Captains
Roy Norden	Bill Hamor	Mike McPherson
	Roger Rosinski	Brian Nardella
		Bruce Nardella
		Al DiPaulo

Captains Brian and Bruce Nardella, Al DiPaulo and Mike McPherson
with Head Coach Roy Norden

SEASON'S RECORD

Beverly	14	Winthrop	8
Beverly	11	Lynn Classical	6
Beverly	24	Danvers	6
Beverly	18	Gloucester	28
Beverly	32	Marblehead	7
Beverly	14	Swampscott	37
Beverly	34	Lynn English	6
Beverly	20	Saugus	7
Beverly	18	Salem	36

6 - 3 - 0

First Row: M. Cauley, J. Underwood, P. Ventresca, C. Manuel, J. Ambrefe, M. Theriault, B. Brewer, C. Hogan, D. Ganey, D. Smith, A. Landers.

Second Row: R. Scott, V. Scarcerella, P. Coyle, B. Doig, C. Eagan, B. Hayes, J. Rice, K. LeCompte.

Third Row: T. Fortunato, R. Herlihy, E. Carrier, A. Innocentti, E. O'Reilly, K. Richardson, B. Roberts, J. Archibald, B. Englehardt, S. Hirschfield, M. Theriault, A. Brown.

Fourth Row: R. Chaney, M. Williams, R. Lewis, B. Petronzio, S. Castellucci, J. Boccia, C. Campbell, M. Allen, J. Grein, R. Baker, J. Connaughton, R. Lee.

Fifth Row: K. Fatuna, S. Bushey, T. Roberts, D. Caverly, T. Barry, S. Barror, D. Gordon, S. Goodwin, K. Boretti, B. Hadden, R. Grein, D. Crowley.

Sixth Row: B. Auld, D. Marshand, B. Carito, S. Hogan, D. Montong, D. Goulbert, R. Sanford, M. McDowell, Fred Abate, D. Weber, R. Tanzella, K. Wooder.

Top Row: Head Coach Nate Cunningham, Ass't. Coaches; D. Chrisos, A. Nizwantowski, B. Manuel, R. Allen, B. Roberts.

1975

<table>
<tr><td>**Head Coach**</td><td>**Ass't Coach**</td><td>**Tri-Captains**</td></tr>
<tr><td>Nate Cunningham</td><td>Ed Nizwantowski
Roger Rosinski</td><td>Mike Theriault
Chris Egan
Ken Richardson</td></tr>
</table>

Tri-captain Mike Theriault Richardson

Tri-captain Chris Egan

Tri-captain Ken

SEASON'S RECORD

Beverly	8	Burlington	34
Beverly	14	Lynn Classical	17 *
Beverly	27	Danvers	6
Beverly	6	Gloucester	38
Beverly	0	Marblehead	3
Beverly	0	Swampscott	7
Beverly	7	Lynn English	6
Beverly	15	Saugus	29
Beverly	6	Winthrop	14
Beverly	14	Salem	22

* Lynn Classical won in overtime with tie-breaker

2 – 8 – 0

(1970)   Welch (22), Allen (80)

(1970) Woods (81) admires a great catch by Drinkwater (21)

(1971)   Dick Whitaker (82) ......Nice catch

(1971)   Bob Connolly (20)...the buck stops here.

(1972)   Wallace (15) hands off to Brown (33)

(1972) Set . . hut ! Brown (33), Harney (66),
B. Nardella (77), Henebury (61), Kinback (58)

(1973)   In the trenches !

(1973) Gary Putur (44)

(1974)   Mike McPherson (20) eyes
his opponent

(1974)   Connaughton (32) displays his stiff-arm

(1975)   Eddie O'Reilly with a lead blocker
against Danvers

(1975)   Manager Bill Brewer likes what he sees

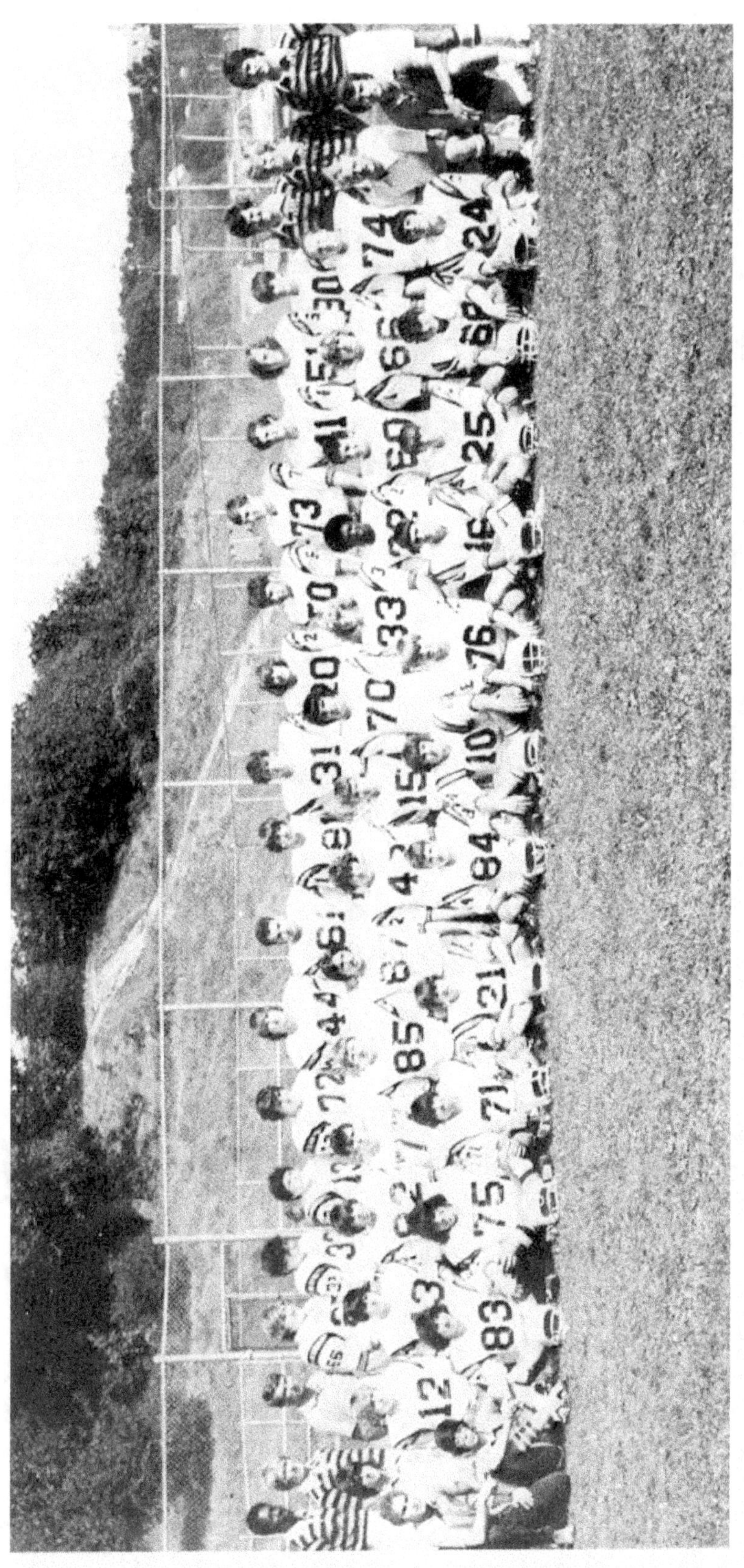

First Row: Coach Modugno, P. Luca, C. Crowley, W. Merrill, M. Servizio, C. Putur, M. Coughlin, B. Hayes, B. Scott, A. Brown, J. Smith, S. Castellucci, B. Petrosino.
Second Row: C. Gilligan, S. Goodwin, T. Barry, R. Chainey, B. Roberts, H. Herlihy, R. Tanzella, J. Rice, K. Boretti, B. Doig, L. Wilcox, R. Baker, R. Modugno, A. Innocenti, A. Landers, Coach Smith, Coach Fournier.
Third Row: Head Coach Cunningham, Coach Nizwantowski, Coach Allen, R. Hadden, J. Connaughton, M. Williams, D. Crowley, E. Carrier, B. Englehart, P. Furnari, K. LeCompte, J. Bradstreet, W. Jordan, D. Gordon, J. Underwood, B. Cahill, S. Bushey, Coach Chrisos, Coach Scanlon, Coach Connaughton.

1976

Assistant Coaches
Modugno
Smith
Fournier
Nizwantowski
Allen
Chrisos
Scanlon
Connaughton

Captains
Jay Rice
Bruce Doig
Ken Boretti

Nate Cunningham, Head Coach

SEASON'S RECORD

Beverly	6	Burlington	0
Beverly	14	Danvers	14
Beverly	2	Gloucester	6
Beverly	6	Marblehead	19
Beverly	0	Swampscott	12
Beverly	14	Lynn English	0
Beverly	19	Saugus	6
Beverly	14	Winthrop	20
Beverly	0	Lynn Classical	21
Beverly	0	Salem	3

3 – 6 – 1

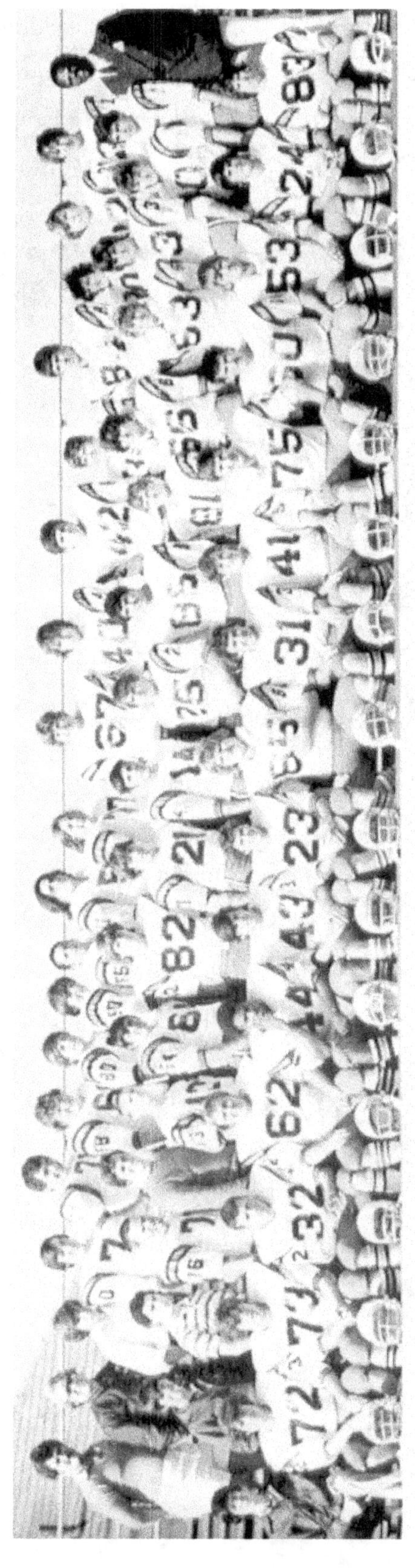

First Row: P. Luca, K. Wolfe, D. MacArthur, J. Connaughton, J. Parker, T. Brooks, T. Barry, G. Ralwing, Captain B. Hadden, Captain K. LeComte, Captain J. Underwood, Captain D. Gordon, D. Caverly, B. Scott, B. Petrosino, B. Yescalis.

Second Row: N. Beaulieau, D. Atwood, J. Bennet, D. Crowley, B. Williams, T. Grein, M. Coughlin, C. Putur, D. LeClair, P. Funari, T. Zambellis, M. Boretti, D. Hilton, K. Cross, B. Gunta, M. Kirrane, B. Gongas, Head Coach Nate Cunningham.

Top Row: Ass't Coach D. Chrisos, Ass't Coach E. Nizwantowski, J. Thomas, L. Vallincourt, T. O'Brien, P. Anderson, M. Jutras, T. Geary, R. Rojas, B. Shea, R. Larcom, J. Norton, F. Kenny, B. Hayes, J. Smith, A. Brown, M. Goldstein, S. Evans, M. Carrier. (Not Pictured – Ass't Coach H. Connaughton, Ass't Coach J. Deluca).

1977

Head Coach	Ass't Coach	Captains
Nate Cunningham	Ed Nizwantowski	Bob Haddon
	Don Chrisson	Kevin LeCompte
	Harry Connaughton	James Underwood
	John Delucca	Dan Gordon

Nate Cunningham, Head Coach explaining a play

SEASON'S RECORD

Beverly	6	Burlington	33
Beverly	6	Gloucester	14
Beverly	15	Marblehead	29
Beverly	6	Swampscott	0 *
Beverly	21	Lynn English	6
Beverly	14	Saugus	28
Beverly	0	Winthrop	6
Beverly	16	Lynn Classical	33
Beverly	6	Danvers	14
Beverly	6	Salem	28

* Swampscott won 19-6 but an inelligible player caused a forfeit

2 - 8 - 0

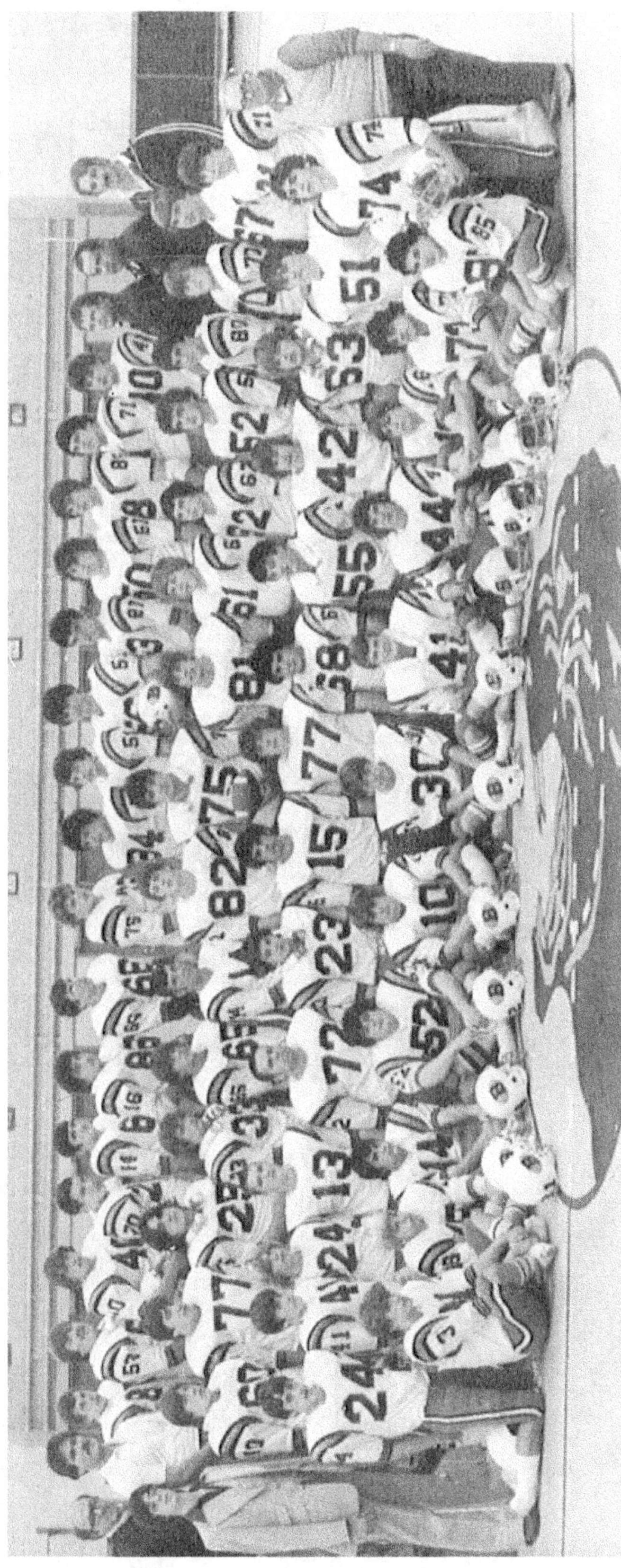

Front Row: T. Major, D. Jutras, D. Halpern, B. Lapka, P. Boretti, P. Dooling, M. Boretti, B. Yescalis, S. Broderick, T. Vitale, K. Counihan.

Second Row: T. Smith, B. Richardson, J. Bartlett, B. Williams, J.W. Bennett, G. Rawding, W. Gongas, S. Worton, J. Paluzzi, G. Shea. K. Rollins. L. Scott, S. James, K. Long.

Third Row: Manager P. Luca, E. J. Estabrook, J. Pelletier, B. Shea, G. Traicoff, T. Geary, D. LeClair, Tri-Captain M. Coughlin, Tri-Captain T. O'Brien, Tri-Captain M. Jutras, M. Smagala, R. Giunta, K. Klein, R. McGurn, D. Nason, J. Norton, C. Putur.

Fourth Row: Ass't Coach T. Divincenzo, Ass't Coach H. Connaughton, J. Geary, B. Richardson, B. Kenney, C. Kinback, T. Grein, C. Ferrante, D. Hilton, P. Anderson, M. Abate, S. Rollins, M. Pascucci, B. Salley, D. Buckley, B. Giunta, A. Cacivvio, P. Cole, Ass't Coach R. Rosinski, Ass't Coach B. Manuel, Head Coach Bill Hamor.

1978

Head Coach	Ass't Coach	Captains
Bill Hamor	T. DiVincenzo	M. Coughlin
	R. Rosinski	T. O'Brien
	H. Connaughton	M. Jutras
	B. Manuel	

From left: W. Gongas, D. LeClair, Tri-captain M. Coughlin, Head Coach Bill Hamor

SEASON'S RECORD

Beverly	0	Burlington	14
Beverly	6	Marblehead	7
Beverly	29	Swampscott	6
Beverly	7	Lynn English	14
Beverly	7	Saugus	12
Beverly	6	Winthrop	21
Beverly	0	Lynn Classical	12
Beverly	6	Danvers	7
Beverly	8	Gloucester	7
Beverly	13	Salem	0

3 – 7 – 0

First Row (Left to Right): W. Shea, W. Gongas, B. Salley, D. Nason, D. Buckley, M. Snagala, A. Vitale, R. Giunta, D. Kline, M. Abate, L. Scott, E. Estabrook, D. Atwood, C. Ferrante, K. Counihan, J. Pelletier.
Second Row: A. Caccivio, B. Hirschfield, J. Paluzzi, S. James, T. Hayes, S. Norton, S. Rollins, R. Young, R. Moroni, S. MaCrae, J. Geary, P. Dooling, B. Richardson, B. Lapka, Bill Hamor (Coach).
Third Row: J. Wright, S. Carleson, C. Coluntino, J. Coan, P. Boretti, M. Pascucci, C. Kinback, T. Major, D. Jutras, D. Deciero, P. Churchyard, J. Bunn, E. Kapantis, Roger Rosinski (Coach).
Back Row: Tony DiVincenzo (Assistant Coach), R. Gorman (Assistant Coach), Harry Connaughton (Assistant Coach), J. Abate, T. Harrington, W. Davis, N. Olsen, M. White, M. Smorgewski, D. Wharton, J. Ward, J. Deluca (Assistant Coach).

1979

Head Coach	Ass't Coach	Captains
Bill Hamor	T. DiVincenzo	Mike Abate
	R. Rosinski	Doug Kline
	H. Connaughton	Rich Giunta
	R. Gorman	

Tri-captain Rich Giunta

Brian Salley

SEASON'S RECORD

Beverly	26	Everett	20
Beverly	18	Swampscott	14
Beverly	20	Lynn English	14
Beverly	0	Saugus	19
Beverly	6	Winthrop	30
Beverly	14	Lynn Classical	40
Beverly	14	Danvers	40
Beverly	0	Gloucester	14
Beverly	14	Marblehead	0
Beverly	20	Salem	21

4 – 6 - 0

First Row (Left to Right): S. Rollins, S. James, J. Silva, P. Boretti, K. Kimback, P. Dooling, C. Shea, R. Moroni, A. Caccivio, B. Lapka, J. Paluzzi, B. Hirschfield, B. Richardson.

Second Row: B. Garcia, S. McRae, L. Wright, T. Harrington, J. Abate, C. Coluntino, D. Pinciaro, D. Wharton, J. Ward, E. Kapantis, M. Smorgewski, B. Davis, J. Malloy.

Third Row: C. Lewis, M. White, J. Maggiacomo, R. Shields, J. Rennick, C. Manuel, D. Maloney, N. Olsen, J. Byrne, T. Conti, D. Smagala, J. Adams, L. Legault, B. Kerr.

Back Row: Coach DiVencenzo, M. Selin, B. Hamor, R. Cunningham, E. McDonald, M. Andreas, D. MacLeod, M. Fall, L. Hackett, K. Rice, M. Carnevale, P. Slabacheski, K. Scotty, Coach Hamor, Coach Rosinski.

(Missing from picture – Co-Captain M. Pascucci, S. Norton, W. Davis)

1980

Head Coach	Ass't Coach	Captains
Bill Hamor	T. DiVincenzo	R. Moroni
	R. Rosinski	M. Pascucci
	H. Connaughton	
	J. DeLucca	

Co-Captain R. Moroni   Coach Bill Hamor   Co-Captain M. Pascucci

SEASON'S RECORD

Beverly	41	Everett	6
Beverly	14	Lynn English	22
Beverly	27	Saugus	0
Beverly	21	Winthrop	0
Beverly	7	Lynn Classical	9
Beverly	8	Danvers	21
Beverly	21	Gloucester	14
Beverly	10	Marblehead	14
Beverly	17	Swampscott	0
Beverly	23	Salem	0

6 – 4 – 0

First Row: T. Harrington, J. Conti, D. Wharton, N. Olson, B. Davis, M. White, J. Abate, J. Ward, C. Coluntino, J. Byrne, M. Smorczewski, E. Kapantis, J. Wright.

Second Row: E. Cook, D. Maloney, M. Guinivan, D. Hackett, B. Hamor, M. Fall, D. Smagala, K. Oteish, R. Shields, J. Maggiacomo, D. MacLeod, B. Garcia, M. Carnevale.

Third Row: K. O'Rourke, C. Dyer, J. Rennicks, C. Manuel, M. Kennedy, B. MacDonald, K. Rice, C. Lewis, S. Pascucci, D. Derragon, J. Slabacheski, B. Mariskelchi, P. Dettore.

Fourth Row: T. Hayes, L. Flynn, J. Mandragorus, J. Miller, J. Putur, G. Cowles, J. Margolis, D. Halpern.

1981

Co-captain Mark White   Co-captain John Abate   Coach Hamor

SEASON'S RECORD

Beverly	18	Everett	0
Beverly	21	Saugus	8
Beverly	0	Winthrop	6
Beverly	18	Lynn Classical	0
Beverly	29	Danvers	12
Beverly	19	Gloucester	6
Beverly	30	Marblehead	13
Beverly	14	Swampscott	0
Beverly	19	Lynn English	14
Beverly	21	Salem	22

8 – 2 – 0

(1976)   SB-81 . . . on two !

(1976) It's yours . . . I don't want it *. . . now go !*

(1977)   Underwood breaks one

(1977) The outlook against Salem is not good

(1978)   Victory is ours !

(1978) A win over Salem and all is forgiven

(1979)   Pass by Gongas (15)

(1979)   Atwood (44) finds a hole

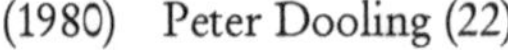

(1980)   Peter Dooling (22)

(1980)   John Abate (13)

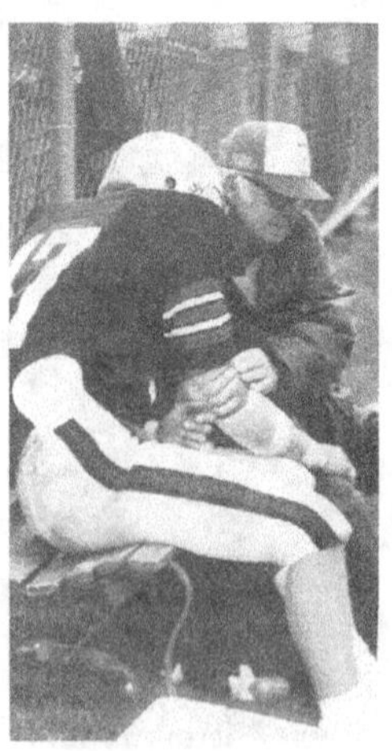

(1981)   Coluntino (10), Ofeish (77)

(1981)   Clammy tending to J. Wright

Front Row: M. Carnevale, D. Hackett, C. Lewis, D. Smagala, D. MacLeod, R. Shields, B. Hamor, M. Andreas, M. Fall, E. Smith, D. Maloney, S. Cecchini, B. Garcia, K. Rice.
Second Row: T. Johnson, J. Mandragorus, K. O'Rourke, J. Mahoney, B. Frost, G. Cowles, J. Putur, J. Miller, D. Dergragon, L. Flynn, C. Matton, P. Slabacheski, S. Barror, Coach DiPaolo.
Third Row: Coach Rosinski, Coach Hamor, D. Mareschauski, J. Ramsdell, C. Burke, P. DiVencenzo, D. Caverly, J. Clarizia, R. DiPasquale, D. Nuccio, J. Margolis, D. Tarr, S. Pascucci, Coach Kaylor.
Fourth Row: Coach Nardella, J. Maggiacomo, J. Mangra, T. Klibanski, C. Cwik, G. Wilcek, H. Geary, M. Lemonte, P. Murphy, T. Burns, T. Flaherty, K. Manuel, E. Wright, G. Corbett, S. Clougy, J. Straw.

1982

Head Coach	Ass't Coach	Captains
Bill Hamor	Roger Rosinski	Randy Shields
	Coach Kaylor	Billy Hamor
	Coach Nardella	
	Al DiPaolo	

Coach Hamor with Co-captains Randy Shields and Billy Hamor

SEASON'S RECORD

Beverly	12	Everett	0
Beverly	14	Winthrop	37
Beverly	8	Lynn Classical	14
Beverly	7	Danvers	6
Beverly	20	Gloucester	7
Beverly	32	Marblehead	6
Beverly	21	Swampscott	14
Beverly	21	Lynn English	0
Beverly	6	Saugus	6
Beverly	6	Salem	15

6 – 3 – 1

First Row: Coach DiPaolo, Dennis Tarr, Bill Center, Jeff Ramsdell, Jeff Slabacheski, Bob Frost, Tri-Captain Steve Pascucci, Tri-Captain Joe Miller, Tri-Captain John Putur, Gary Cowles, Sean Barror, Pat Murphy, Chris Matton, Dave Nuccio, Len Flynn, Kurt O'Rourke, Jeff Margolis, Rick DePasquale.

Second Row: Coach Kaylor, Coach Modugno, Coach Brown, Ron Guinta, Scott Matton, Scott Durgin, Hal Geary, Tim Flaherty, Ed Wright, Tom Hayes, Nick Papandreou, Brad Lord, Todd Klibansky, Matt Wilczek, Steve Kluge, Coach Hamor, Coach Richardson, Coach Allen, Coach Rosinski.

Third Row: Phil Pascucci, Bob Guay, Pat Barror, Dave Mandragouras, Jeff Silva, Brenden O'Donoghue, Dana Trembly, Troy Ward, Fred Cwik, Pat Murray, John Snow.

Fourth Row: Ray Clemens, Jeff Bryson, Jason Toussaint, John Morency, Chris Peters, Chris Brown, Frank Presutti, Jeff Pavia, Tim Wolfe, Dave Wright, Jason Straw, Jim Cecchini, Spenser MacDonald, and John Mandragouras. (Missing from photo: Ed Moulton, Tim Byrne, Dave Wright, Jason Straw, Jim Cecchini, Spenser MacDonald, and John Mandragouras)

1983

Head Coach	Ass't Coach	Captains
Bill Hamor	Roger Rosinski	Joseph Miller
	John Allen	Steve Pascucci
	Steve Richardson	John Putur
	Dave Modugno	
	Al DiPaolo	
	Coach Kaylor	
	Coach Brown	

Tri-Captain Steve Pascucci

Scott Durgin

SEASON'S RECORD

Beverly	38	Everett	8
Beverly	19	Lynn Classical	12
Beverly	21	Danvers	35
Beverly	12	Gloucester	6
Beverly	45	Marblehead	6
Beverly	21	Swampscott	12
Beverly	17	Lynn English	0
Beverly	6	Saugus	12
Beverly	13	Winthrop	13 *
Beverly	6	Salem	8

* Winthrop's 33 game winning streak stopped with tie game

6 – 3 – 1

First Row: M. Bates, K. Manuel, T. Klibansky, S. Durgin, Tri-Captain B. Lord, Tri-Captain N. Papandreou, Tri-Captain T. Flaherty, H. Geary, G. Wilczek, J. Straw, M. Schlegel, R. Guinta, E. Wright.
Second Row: R. Bowden, D. Pascucci, S. Kluge, P. Murray, F. Cwik, B. Wescott, T. Byrne, G. Waddell, P. Barror, M. Raymond, W. Clark.
Third Row: T. Ward, J. Shairs, J. Morency, J. Bryson, B. Guay, J. Cecchini, C. Brown, C. Peters, D. Mandragouras, F. Persutti.
Fourth Row: J. Pavia, B. Stavis, A. Morency, D. Margolis, C. Guyer, S. Stanwood, J. Bennett, S. Bernard.
Fifth Row: J. Carratu, S. Reilly, D. Winters, S. Walker, D. Belisle, C. Waisenen. (Missing from picture: Brian Hadden)

1984

Tri-captains Tim Flaherty, Brad Lord, and Nick Papandreou with Coach Bill Hamor

SEASON'S RECORD

Beverly	27	Everett	6
Beverly	37	Danvers	13
Beverly	14	Gloucester	18
Beverly	16	Marblehead	6
Beverly	35	Swampscott	15
Beverly	34	Lynn English	0
Beverly	22	Saugus	8
Beverly	28	Winthrop	7
Beverly	16	Lynn Classical	6
Beverly	28	Salem	14

9 – 1 – 0

First Row: Coach Al Harrington, Frank Presutti, Dave Mandragouras, Chris Peters, Tri-Captain Pat Barror, Tri-Captain Chris Brown, Tri-Captain Duke Pascucci, Troy Ward, Jeff Bryson, Bob Guay, Jeff Pavia, John Morency, Jim Cecchini, John Snow.
Second Row: Coach Roger Rosinski, Craig Walker, Jeff Bennett, Scott Bernard, Chuck Palmer, Dave Caverly, Bernie Stavis, Andrew Morency, Gary Main, John Shairs, Bruce Burgess, Mike Raymond, David Winter, Bob Naylor, Jim Petrosino, Head Coach Bill hanor.
Third Row: Eric Kausel, Peter Bowden, Wayne Clark, Dana Margolis, Charlie Guyer, Scott Stanwood, John Smith, Mike Polinski, Shawn Reilly, David James. Equiptment Manager Leroy 'Red' Hutt.
Fourth Row: Kevin Lang, Sean Gallager, Jeff Nicolo, Marc LeClair, John Daras, Dick Donahue, Mark Lyons, Kevin Whalen, Scott Soucy, John Sidman.

1985

Head Coach	Ass't Coach	Captains
Bill Hamor	Roger Rosinski	Pat Barror
	Al Harrington	Chris Brown
		Duke Pascucci

Co-Captains, l to r, Pat Barror, Chris Brown, Duke Pascucci

SEASON'S RECORD

Beverly	33	Everett	16
Beverly	12	Gloucester	0
Beverly	8	Marblehead	7
Beverly	7	Swampscott	24
Beverly	3	Lynn English	0
Beverly	29	Saugus	22
Beverly	21	Winthrop	14
Beverly	30	Lynn Classical	13
Beverly	34	Danvers	12
Beverly	14	Salem	6

9 – 1 - 0

Northeast Conference Champions

First Row: Coach A. DiPaolo, Trainer R. Puopolo, Equiptment Manager Leroy 'Red' Hutt, Tri-Captain A. Morency, Tri-Captain K. Whalen, Tri-Captain P. Bowden, Coach J. Allen, Head Coach Bill Hamor, Coach R. Rosinski.

Second Row: D. Margolis, C. Palmer, M. Raymond, C. Guyer, J. Lesalva, B. Stavis, J. Shairs, S. Bernard, J. Bennett, S. Stanwood, W. Clark.

Third Row: K. Rivers, D. Lien, G. Main, B. Pompey, R. Naylor, R. Dunn, J. Petrosino, B. Burgess, J. Cirinna, C. Walker.

Fourth Row: D. Fielding, M. LeClair, K. Lang, J. Daras, D. Manuel, D. Nugent, J. Sidman, D. Donahue, S. Galazia, W. Beecher, M. Palinski.

Fifth Row: D. Pzenny, M. Arciaga, D. Peters, J. Shairs, E. Kausel, T. Gallager, V. Morgan, J. Young, M. Stacey, J. Richards.

Top Row: K. Clary, T. Richards, R. White, B. Richards, D. Jalbert, P. Consalazio, J. Mansfield, S. Costa, L. Hamor, W. Trefrey, K. Piecewicz.

1986

<table>
<tr><td>**Head Coach**</td><td>**Ass't Coach**</td><td>**Captains**</td></tr>
<tr><td>Bill Hamor</td><td>Roger Rosinski</td><td>Andrew Morency</td></tr>
<tr><td></td><td>Al DiPaolo</td><td>Kevin Whalen</td></tr>
<tr><td></td><td>John Allen</td><td>Peter Bowden</td></tr>
</table>

Brain Trust

Coaches, from left, John Allen, Al Harrington, Al DiPaolo, Head coach Bill Hamor and Roger Rosinski

SEASON'S RECORD

Beverly	6	Everett	0
Beverly	7	Marblehead	14
Beverly	12	Swampscott	6
Beverly	33	Lynn English	6
Beverly	44	Saugus	6
Beverly	7	Winthrop	14
Beverly	42	Lynn Classical	26
Beverly	27	Danvers	14
Beverly	20	Gloucester	11
Beverly	6	Salem	33

7 – 3 – 0

First Row: (Left to right) : Coach A. DiPaolo, Equipment Manager Leroy 'Red' Hutt, Head Coach Bill Hamor, Tri-Captain M. Palinski, Tri-Captain M. LeClair, Tri-Captain D. Donahue, Coach R. Rosinski, Trainer R. Puopolo.

Second Row: T. Gallager, J. Sidman, W. Beecher, E. Kausel, S. Galazia, D. Pzenny, D. Nugent, M. Koloski, K. Lang, J. Daras.

Third Row: R. Carrol, D. Peters, J. Shairs, M. Arciaga, M. Stacey.

Fourth Row: B. Palinski, B. Richards, P. Consolazio, K. Piecewicz, K. Rivers, W. Trefry, R. White, T. Kyger, Y. Tran, E. Levasseur, E. Cole.

Top Row: C. Lantz, A. Mott, J. Tucker, P. Wallace, M. Toulouse, J. St Arneault. T. Maloney, S. Cowles, B. Boretti, S. Shairs, B. Consolazio. R. Phillips.

169

1987

Head Coach	Ass't Coach	Captains
Bill Hamor	Roger Rosinski	Mike Palinski
	Al DiPaolo	Marc LeClair
	John Allen	Dick Donahue

Tri-captains Mike Palinski, Marc LeClair and Dick Donahue

SEASON'S RECORD

Beverly	7	Everett	21
Beverly	7	Swampscott	6
Beverly	10	Lynn English	0
Beverly	21	Saugus	0
Beverly	21	Winthrop	2
Beverly	25	Lynn Classical	15
Beverly	14	Danvers	10
Beverly	12	Gloucester	40
Beverly	14	Marblehead	12
Beverly	19	Salem	14

8 – 2 – 0

(1982)   Let's get it on !

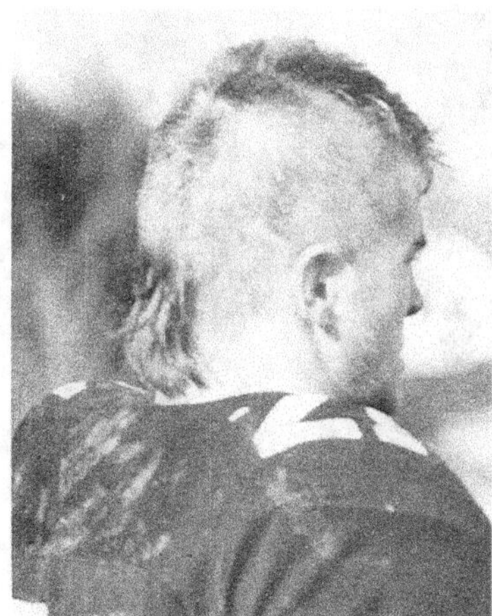

(1982)   A sign of the times !

(1983)   Joe Miller (44) gets stuffed !

(1983)   Hut . . . . hut !

(1984)   Durgin (22) say's 'Get out of my way!'

(1984) Flaherty (33) with clear sail'n

(1985)   Tough and muddy, but we still beat Salem   (1985)   Pat Barror (11) just gets the pass off

(1986)   Rock . . . paper . . . scissor   (1986)   Airborne !

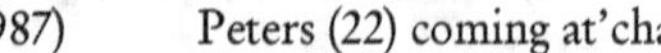

(1987)   Peters (22) coming at'cha   (1987)   LeClair (17) breaks the huddle

First Row (Left to Right): Coach Rosinski, Coach DiPaolo, L. Hamor, S. Costa, W. Trefry, Coach Hamor, Equipment Manager 'Red' Hutt.

Second Row: R. White, P. Consolazio, B. Richards, J. Richard, M. Stacey, J. Young, K. Rivers, K. Piecewicz, D. Jalbert, M. Arciaga, J. Shairs, D. Peters, R. Forrest.

Third Row: C. Lantz, B. Badger, A. Desany, B. Consolazio, J. Tucker, T. Maloney, P. Wallace, S. Shairs, A. Mott, B. Palinski, E. Coll, Ian Carr.

Fourth Row: E. Levasseur, J. Widfeldt, M. Gillespie, B. Johnson, J. Corroca, C. Servizio, S. Hyland, M. Soucy, B. Boretti, S. Cowles, D. Bowden.

Fifth Row: S. Roid, D. York, D. Arena, J. Vaccaro, R. Phillips, J. St. Arneault, C. Fontaine.

1988

Head Coach Bill Hamor with Tri-Captains: Steve Costa, L Hamor, W. Trefry

SEASON'S RECORD

Beverly	41	Everett	16
Beverly	23	Lynn English	12
Beverly	34	Saugus	0
Beverly	32	Winthrop	7
Beverly	43	Lynn Classical	28
Beverly	37	Danvers	7
Beverly	28	Gloucester	14
Beverly	8	Marblehead	7
Beverly	34	Swampscott	14
Beverly	14	Salem	6

10 – 0 – 0

UNDEFEATED - UNTIED

SUPERBOWL

Beverly	*6*	*Dracut*	*23*

First Row: L. Hutt, ________, Coach Bill Hamor, B. Boretti, A. Mott, T. Maloney, Coach Rosinski, Coach Toner, Coach Allen, Coach DiPaolo.
Second Row: D. Arena, B. Palinski, S. Cowles, B. Consolazio, C. Vincent, B. Wallace, J. Tucker, S. Shairs, M. Toulouse, E. Cole, C. Lantz.
Third Row: T. Fields, J. Widfeldt, M. Marino, A. Sutton, S. Trenquina, S. Hyland, R. Phillips, E. Levasseur, J. Vaccaro, D. Boden, E. Abramson, J. Corroco, M. Gillespie.
Fourth Row: J. St. Arneault, ________, T. Guarino, G. Cerrone, M. Heckman, D. Castaluccio, (?) Potzin, E. Shairs, M. Cotraro, T. Coleman, M. DiDonato.
Fifth Row: B. Cotoia, M. Lewis, J. Coletti, M. Murphy, C. Fiore.

1989

Head Coach	Ass't Coach	Captains
Bill Hamor	Roger Rosinski	Brett Boretti
	Al DiPaolo	Tom Maloney
	John Allen	Adam Mott
	Mark Toner	

Coach Hamor talks things over with Tri-captain Brett Boretti

SEASON'S RECORD

Beverly	22	Everett	26
Beverly	21	Saugus	7
Beverly	28	Winthrop	7
Beverly	32	Lynn Classical	0
Beverly	35	Danvers	12
Beverly	20	Gloucester	13
Beverly	37	Marblehead	0
Beverly	20	Swampscott	14
Beverly	7	Lynn English	28
Beverly	8	Salem	20

7 - 3 - 0

First Row: Equipment Manager 'Red' Hutt, Trainer A. Flaherty, Captain B. Boden, Captain S. Hyland, Captain J. Widfeldt, Head Coach R. Rosinski, Coach Harrington, Coach Gallagher, Coach Ingram.
Second Row: M. Gillespie, J. Vaccaro, J. St Arneault, T. Field, S. Trenquina, R. Phillips, D. Arena, E. Levasseur, M. Marino.
Third Row: M. Heckman, C. Fiore, E. Shairs, M. Murphy, T. Geary, T. Guarino, G. Cirone, A. Doty, B. Catoia.
Fourth Row: M. DiDinado, J. Coletti, L. Debussion, J. Barricelli, M. Gerrish, K. Costain, J. Mower, C. Viel, A. Riddle, L. Sharamitaro.
Fifth Row: T. Murphy, B. Boden, P. Grossman, M. Mosco, J. Vagos, J. Heckman, T. L'Italien, D. Russo, A. MacLeod, A. Belmonte, R. Meagher, M. Sciucco.

1990

HEAD COACH	ASS'T COACHES	CAPTAINS
Roger Rosinski	Peter Harrington	Derrick Boden
	Paul Ingrams	Jeremy Widfeldt
	Paul Harrington	Scott Hyland
	Sean Gallagher	
	Chris Frates	
	Steve Kaylor	

Coach Rosinski with, from left, Tri-captains S. Hyland, J. Widfeldt, and D. Boden

SEASON'S RECORD

Beverly	0	Everett	7
Beverly	30	Winthrop	0
Beverly	26	Lynn Classical	0
Beverly	35	Danvers	12
Beverly	29	Gloucester	13
Beverly	12	Marblehead	7
Beverly	9	Swampscott	14
Beverly	14	Lynn English	18
Beverly	6	Saugus	29
Beverly	13	Salem	6

6 – 4 – 0

First Row (Left to right) : Coach P. Harrington, Coach A. Morency, Coach S. Gallagher, C. Fiore, A. Garry, M. Murphy, M. Heckman, B. Cotoia, (Captain) J. Coletti, (Captain) T. Guarino, (Captain) E. Shairs, M. Cotraro, M. DiDonato, Head Coach Roger Rosinski, Coach P. Harrington, Coach J. Allen.
Second Row: M. Sciucco, L. Dubuisson, P. Grossman, T. Murphy, D. Russo, A. Macleod, B. Boden, C. Viel, T. L'Italian, A. Riddle, K. Costain, J. Mower, J. Heckman, J. Barricelli, C. Gadbois, R. Meagher, M. Gerrish, A. Belmonte.
Top Row: J. Parelli, E. Richard, J. McAlpine, D. Costa, D. Cowles, T. Kaylor, T. Fisher, J. Koen, V. Garry, J. Roccio, J. Pavia, C. Elario, S. Kagels, M. Burke, B. Badger, T. Fessenden, S. Vesely.

1991

HEAD COACH	ASS'T COACHES	CAPTAINS
Roger Rosinski	Peter Harrington	J. Coletti
	Andrew Morency	T. Guarino
	Paul Harrington	E. Shairs
	Sean Gallagher	
	John Allen	

From left: Ass't coach John Allen, Head coach Roger Rosinski, Athletic Director Bill Hamor and Ass't coach P. Harrington

SEASON'S RECORD

Beverly	21	Peabody	6
Beverly	20	Everett	8
Beverly	12	Lynn Classical	20
Beverly	13	Danvers	7
Beverly	13	Gloucester	34
Beverly	31	Marblehead	15
Beverly	28	Swampscott	0
Beverly	14	Lynn English	21
Beverly	32	Saugus	0
Beverly	38	Winthrop	7
Beverly	16	Salem	20

7 – 4 – 0

First Row (Left to right) : Coach P. Harrington, Coach H. Connaughton, Coach A. Morency, Captain P. Grossman, Captain T. Murphy, Captain K. Costain, Captain C. Viel, M. Sciucco, R. Norden, A. Rieman, B. Riddle.
Second Row: J. Barricelli, J. Ciarnataro, T. L'Italian, B. Boden, A. MacLeod, C. Gadbois, M. Gerrish, A. Belmonte, A. Riddle, D. Russo, L. Dubuisson, J. Broderick, R. Meagher, J. Heckman.
Third Row: B. Badger, M. Burke, S. Vesely, J. Parelli, D. Cowles, D. Costa, C. Elario, A. Bousquet, S. Kagels, J. Koen, J. Roccio.
Fourth Row: D. Toulouse, D. Purdy, J. Finney, M. Boden, V. Garry, J. Carlson, T. Kaylor, E. Richard, T. Murphy, D. Rafter, J. Aucone, M. Abisanra.
Top Row: B. Nicoll, K. Beaulieu, J. Peters, T. Conant, E. Mantevecchi, C. Gagnon, J. Hodgson, M. Gillespie, E. Knowlton, J. Garry.

1992

Captains: T. Murphy, P. Grossman, C. Viel, M. Sciucco, K. Costain

SEASON'S RECORD

Beverly	32	Everett	8
Beverly	0	Danvers	9
Beverly	20	Gloucester	8
Beverly	0	Swampscott	6
Beverly	42	Marblehead	7
Beverly	40	Saugus	6
Beverly	32	Lynn Classical	0
Beverly	6	Winthrop	20
Beverly	11	Lynn English	30
Beverly	6	Salem	0

6 – 4 – 0

(Listing of players only)

First Row: J. Roccio. Captain D. Costa. Captain T. Kaylor. D. Purdy.

Second Row: J. Carlson, D. Cowles. S. Vesley. J. Parelli. S. Kagels. E. Richard. C. Elario. B. Badger.

Third Row: K. Beaulieu. J. Peters. B. Boden. T. Conant. P. Hennessey. J. Hodgson. E. Knowlton.

Fourth Row: M. Gillespie. D. Toulouse. D. Rafter. T. Murphy. B. Nichols. J. Aucone. J. Garry. E. Brillant.

Fifth Row: J. Sullivan. J. Eswara. M. Barricelli. J. Viel. C. Essley. J. Vuylstelce. P. Henebury. A. Gooley. B. Barror.

Top Row: A. Fox. S. Carr. J. Fultz. A. Kemp. J. Copelas. W. Pattepron. D. Sauvageau. J. Smorczewski.

1993

HEAD COACH	ASS'T COACHES	CAPTAINS
Roger Rosinski	Peter Harrington	Tom Kaylor
	Andrew Morency	David Costa
	Robert Almeida	

Co-Captains

David Costa   Tom Kaylor

SEASON'S RECORD

Beverly	25	Everett	13
Beverly	26	Gloucester	0
Beverly	41	Marblehead	6
Beverly	32	Swampscott	6
Beverly	42	Lynn English	7
Beverly	50	Saugus	24
Beverly	6	Winthrop	21
Beverly	0	Lynn Classical	27
Beverly	0	Danvers	7
Beverly	20	Salem	16

7 – 3 – 0

(1988) Shairs hands off to Peters

(1988) Nice block . . but is it legal?

(1989)   Dan Arena (16) cuts left

(1989)   Brett Boretti (31) reaching

for that extra yard

(1990)   Scott Hyland (23) looking to connect

(1990)   Guarino (44) with no place to go

(1991)　　　Coin toss . . . heads or tails?

(1991)　Cotraro with running room

(1992)　　　No hole there . . .

(1992)　　　Let go of my jersey !

(1993)　　　Goal line success

(1993)　　　This is as far as you go . . .

First Row: Coach R. Rosinski, Trainer A. Remon, Equipment Manager L. Hutt, Captain T. Conant, Captain M. Boden, Captain T. Murphy, Coach A. Morency.
Second Row: J. Hodgson, F. Ortiz, J. Peters, K. Beaulieu, D. Rafter, D. Toulouse, E. Knowlton, E. Brillant, J. Garry.
Third Row: C. Essler, P. Henebury, K. Berger, P. Hennessey, M. Abisamra, B. Barror, L. Smith, J. Smorczewski, J. Viel
Fourth Row: S. Carr, J. Eswara, A. Kemp, A. Fox, J. Fultz, W. Patterson, J. Copelas, M. Barricelli, R. Sheridan.
Top Row: S. Martin, R. Smith, S. Rafter, T. Fitzpatrick, K. Sewyck, P. McKenna, J. Belmonte, L. Berger

1994

HEAD COACH	ASS'T COACHES	CAPTAINS
Roger Rosinski	Peter Harrington	Terry Conant
	Andrew Morency	Matt Boden
	Robert Almeida	Tim Murphy

Captains (l to r): Terry Conant, Matt Boden, Tim Murphy

SEASON'S RECORD

Beverly	0	Everett	24
Beverly	26	Marblehead	21
Beverly	10	Swampscott	20
Beverly	37	Lynn English	20
Beverly	30	Saugus	0
Beverly	35	Winthrop	7
Beverly	35	Lynn Classical	2
Beverly	41	Danvers	7
Beverly	41	Gloucester	0
Beverly	13	Salem	17

7 – 3 - 0

First Row (Left to Right): J. Copelas, M. Barricelli (Co-Captain), A. Fox, P. Henebury (Co-Captain), K. Berger.

Second Row: J. Sullivan, E. Dodge, B. Barror, J. Eswara, C. Essler, S. Carr, D. Sauvageau, M. Hart, R. Caverly, A. Gooley, A. Kemp, W. Patterson.

Third Row: T. Fitzpatrick, S. Martin, J. Belmonte, S. Rafler, R. Smith, K. Sewyck, W. St Preaux, S. Dullea, M. Osborne.

Fourth Row: N. Bochynski, G. Andrews, B. Ronci, N. Kennedy, S. Bahal, B. Hubis, B. Soucy, J. Nichols.

Fifth Row: M. Henebury, D. Whitaker, D. Tinson, S. Ward, J. Alphen, L. Knowlton, D. MacDonald.

Back Row: L. Hutt (Manager), A. Flaherty (Trainer), D. Wilbur (Coach), R. Rosinski (Head Coach), H. Connaughton (Coach), A. Morency (Coach), P. Harrington (Coach).

1995

<u>HEAD</u> <u>COACH</u>	ASS'T COACHES	CAPTAINS
Roger Rosinski	Peter Harrington	Matt Barricelli
	Andrew Morency	Pat Henebury
	Harry Connaughton	
	D. Wilber	

Co-Captain Matt Barricelli Henebury

Coach Rosinski confers

with Henebury

Co-Captain Pat

SEASON'S RECORD

Beverly	6	Acton-Boxboro	35
Beverly	6	Swampscott	35
Beverly	15	Lynn English	10
Beverly	7	Saugus	20
Beverly	12	Winthrop	7
Beverly	21	Lynn Classical	0
Beverly	29	Danvers	7
Beverly	25	Gloucester	28
Beverly	39	Marblehead	0
Beverly	6	Salem	6

5 – 4 – 1

First Row: R. Smith, M. Osborne, K. Sewyck, Captain S. Rafter, Captain J. Belmonte, Captain S. Martin, J. Ditchek, T. Fitzpatrick, V. Demel, P. Roberts.
Second Row: B. Hubis, R. Ronci, S. Bahal, S. Ward, N. Kennedy, R. Singleton, R. Whitaker, S. Dullea, M. Henebury, U. LaFontaint.
Third Row: J. Costa, J. Levesque, G. Andrews, W. St. Preaux, D. Timson, A. Hall, L. Knowlton, N. Bochynski, D. MacDonald.
Fourth Row: J. Terry, D. Thomas, N. Grein, A. Page, M. Amatucci, A. Bartlett, J. Shairs, C. Harrison, N. Pelletier, M. Goldberg.
Fifth Row: Manager 'Red' Hutt, Trainer A. Flaherty, Coach D. Wilbur, Coach A. Morency, Coach H. Connaughton, Head Coach R. Rosinski, Coach P. Harrington.

1996

HEAD COACH	ASS'T COACHES	CAPTAINS
Roger Rosinski	Peter Harrington	S. Rafter
	Andrew Morency	J. Belmonte
	Harry Connaughton	S. Martin
	D. Wilber	

Coach Rosinski with Tri-captains, from left, J. Belmonte, S. Martin, S. Rafter

SEASON'S RECORD

Beverly	14	Peabody	42
Beverly	24	Acton-Boxboro	15
Beverly	6	Lynn English	19
Beverly	21	Saugus	12
Beverly	15	Winthrop	35
Beverly	25	Lynn Classical	33
Beverly	6	Danvers	14
Beverly	16	Gloucester	39
Beverly	13	Marblehead	19
Beverly	6	Swampscott	46
Beverly	21	Salem	22

2 – 9 – 0

First Row: D. MacDonald, L. Knowlton, B. Hubis, Captain W. St. Preux, Captain N. Kennedy, Captain D. Timpson, Captain B. Ronci, S. Bahal, N. Bochinski, S. Ward.

Second Row: A. McGee, J. Wilson, A. Bartlett, D. Thomas, A. Page, J. Shairs, M. Amatucci, J. Levesque, N. Pelletier, M. Goldenberg, C. Harrington

Third Row: Head Coach R. Rosinski, Coach P. Harrington, Coach Maggiacomo, Coach Clark, J. Sullivan, S. Kaylor, M. Krouse, M. Ventresca, R. Hirshfield, M. Smith, I. Chase, J. Keating, B. Vanderbogart, P. Fontaine, E. Moore, C. Holak, P. McGinnity, Coach Hamor, Coach Damarco, Coach Wilber.

1997

HEAD COACH	ASS'T COACHES	CAPTAINS
Roger Rosinski	Harrington	Webster St. Preux
	Maggiacomo	Nathan Kennedy
	Clark	Dave Timpson
	Wilber	Bob Ronci
	Hamor	
	DeMarco	

Front row: Captains (l to r): Nathan Kennedy and Webster St. Preux,
*Back row:*Coach Rosinski flanked by (l to r) Captains David Timson and Robert Ronci.

SEASON'S RECORD

Beverly	7	Peabody	20
Beverly	27	Acton-Boxboro	31
Beverly	12	Saugus	12
Beverly	31	Winthrop	21
Beverly	27	Lynn Classical	8
Beverly	31	Danvers	8
Beverly	6	Gloucester	35
Beverly	27	Marblehead	0
Beverly	6	Swampscott	26
Beverly	6	Lynn English	8
Beverly	34	Salem	22

5 – 5 – 1

First Row: D. Thomas. J. Levesque. N. Pelletier. J. Shairs. M. Goldenberg. A. Bartlett. C. Harrison.

Second Row: Coach D. Wilber. Coach J. DeMarco. J. Wilson. N. Grein. A. Page. C. Ambrose. M. Annatucci. Coach J. Maggiacomo. Coach R. Rosinski.

Third Row: J. Keating. B. Vanderbogert. J. Sullivan. I. Chase. M. Smith. C. Harrington. P. Fontaine.

Fourth Row: R. Stewart. D. Roccio. R. Hirschfeld. P. Belmonte. S. Streiff. E. Moore. M. Ventresca. B. Glynn. R. Davenport.

Top Row: E. Conant. B. Osborne. S. Lang. P. Doyle. S. Oxton. M. Gall.

1998

HEAD COACH	ASS'T COACHES	CAPTAINS
Roger Rosinski	Maggiacomo	M. Goldenberg
	DeMarco	N. Pelletier
	Wilber	J. Shairs

Coach Rosinski with Tri-captains M. Goldenberg, N. Pelletier, and J. Shairs

SEASON'S RECORD

Beverly	15	Acton-Boxboro	14
Beverly	34	Winthrop	3
Beverly	32	Lynn Classical	20
Beverly	36	Danvers	8
Beverly	22	Gloucester	38
Beverly	28	Marblehead	0
Beverly	32	Swampscott	8
Beverly	28	Lynn English	13
Beverly	37	Saugus	6
Beverly	8	Salem	7

9 – 1 – 0

First Row: Brian VanDeBogert, Jared Sullivan, Juan Garcia, Mike Ventresca, Corey Paul Harrington, Eugene Moore, Mike Smith, Ben Garry, Pete Fontaine, Justin Keating, Jason Gaudenzi, Shawn Streiff, Ryan Hirschfeld.

Second Row: Matt Davidson, Kevin Kaylor, Chris Klessens, Steven Lang, Mike Gall, Pat Belmonte, Matt Rooney, Jason Kusiak, Ryan Comb, Chris O'Neil, Scott Gambale, Jake Chadwell, Richard Caccia, Chris Stackpole, Pat Doyle.

Back Row: Head Coach R. Rosinski, Ass't Coach Wilbur, Charles Gerrior, Carlos Ortiz, Kevin Downer, Craig Bowman, David Roccio, Eric Conant, Nick Saraglow, Luke Vuylsteke, Patrick Willey, Matt Bray, Mark MacDonald, Reid Davenport, Scott Oxton, John Palm, Ass't Coach Mullen, Ass't Coach Trayster.

1999

HEAD COACH	ASS'T COACHES	CAPTAINS
Roger Rosinski	Mullen	Mike Smith
	Trayster	Eugene Moore
	Wilber	Corey Harrington

Coach Rosinski with Co-Captains: Mike Smith, Eugene Moore, Corey Harrington

SEASON'S RECORD

Beverly	7	Acton-Boxboro	13
Beverly	10	Lynn Classical	14
Beverly	40	Danvers	20
Beverly	14	Gloucester	28
Beverly	42	Marblehead	12
Beverly	32	Swampscott	20
Beverly	13	Lynn English	12
Beverly	38	Saugus	6
Beverly	31	Winthrop	7
Beverly	0	Salem	14

6 – 4 – 0

(1994)   Who's got the ball?

(1994)   Touchdown celebration!

(1995)   Touchdown !!

(1995) End zone celebration – B. Barror (78), Seth Carr (44)

(1996)   No . . . you don't !

(1996)   Now, this is what we're going to do . . .

(1997)   We're ready . . . bring it on!

(1997)   Handoff to St. Preux

(1998)   Shairs goes to the air . . .

(1998)   Moore was hard to bring down

(1999)   Corey Harrington snags one

(1999)   Eugene Moore begins a runback

Potpourri

B.H.S. Coaches
1900 – 1999

Year	Coach	Notable Highlights
1900 – 1902	None *	
1903	F. W. C. Foster	
1904	Carl Iverson	
1905	Doc Standley	
1906 – 1912	B. H. Squires	Undefeated - 1908
1913	Charlie Sisson	
1914 – 1917	Jack MacDonald	Undefeated – 1915
1918	No team due to World War I	
1919 - 1920	William McKenzie	
1921 – 1923	Elmer Fitzgibbons	
1924 – 1925	Marty Donovan	
1926 - 1927	Hubber Collins	
1928 – 1930	Steve Patten	
1931 – 1935	Bodger Carroll	
1936 – 1938	Ellsworth Richardson	
1939	Bill Foley	
1940 – 1942	Nick Morris	
1943	Henry Toczylowski	
1944 – 1958	Charlie Walsh	Un-un 1948 / Undefeated 1958
1959 – 1974	Roy Norden	Undefeated-untied 1960 & 1964
1975 – 1977	Nate Cunningham	
1978 – 1989	Bill Hamor	N.E. Conf. Champ '85 – Un-un 1988
1990 – 1999	Roger Rosinski **	

* Prior to 1903, captain of the team more or less coached the team   ** Coached through 2002.

Beverly High School Sports Hall of Fame

2003

Mel Deveau (1929)	Jeff Forbes (1960)
Flavio Tosi (1929)	Rocky Ellis (1962)
Charlie Pelonzi (1933)	Walter Grant (1962)
Hugh Nelson (1937)	Bill Norris (1962)
Robbie Robinson (1946)	Bippy Manuel (1963)
Sandy Kessaris (1949)	Dave Tomeo (1965)
Bill Ransom (1950)	Stu Irving (1969)
Fred Hammond (1953)	Bill Gilligan (1972)
Charlie Woods (1958)	Charlie Walsh (Coach)
Bill Hamor (1959)	Roy Norden (Coach)
Emily Morency (1959)	

2004

Al Turner (1927)	Jay Rice (1977)
Charlie Manuel (1952)	Julie Burke Peterson (1978)
Fred Carnevale (1955)	Kelly LeComte (1982)
Harry Ball, Jr (1956)	Jeff Andrews (1992)
Tony DiVincenzo (1959)	Rick Mazzei (Coach)
Mike Tomeo (1959)	George Taylor (Coach)
Roger Pierce (1962)	Clarence 'Clammy' Foster (Trainer)
Mike Gilligan (1966)	

2005

Douglas L. Raymond (1933)	Bob Norris (1965)
Lucien Belanger (1935)	Mark Murray (1966)
Mickey Abate (1950)	John Wright (1968)
Fred Bucci (1951)	Todd Lampert (1969)
Bob Mattson (1952)	Jane K. Frost (1975)
Earl Carter (1958)	Darla Parisi (1982)
Gordon Reid (1959)	Steve Pascucci (1984)
John Ryan (1959)	George Kinnaly (Coach)
John Carratu (1961)	

2006

Jack Heaphy (1917)	Doug Vigliotta (1983)
Bill Whalen (1958)	Brett Boretti (1990)
Bruce Butterworth (1965)	Adam Mott (1990)
Brian Reinhold (1972)	Ernie Faulkner (1990)
John Chludzenski (1975)	Sarah McGrath Hagge (1993)
Deb O'Reilly Kline (1979)	Leroy 'Red' Hutt (Manager)

FRED M. BUCCI SCHOLARSHIP

The Fred M. Bucci Memorial Scholarship has been presented to a deserving senior BHS football player each year since 1945 by the Beverly Sports Club, now known as the Beverly Football Boosters Sports Club.

The scholarship award recipients and the colleges they chose to attend are:

Year	Recipient	College		Year	Recipient	College
1945	John Dooling	Bates		1973	Tim Harney	U Mass.
1946	Robert Robinson	Georgia Tech		1974	Don Spiridigliozzi	Mass. Maritime
1947	Wendall Mason	Tufts		1975	Mike Bushey	Bentley
1948	George Sunderland	Brown		1976	Chris Egan	Bowdoin
1949	Kenneth Kessaris	Brown		1977	Mike Williams	Bridgewater St
1950	George Accomando	Univ. of R.I.		1978	Andrew Brown	Bowdoin
1951	Richard Carr	Columbia		1979	Dennis LeClair	Dartmouth
1952	Robert Mattson	Tufts		1980	Richard Guinta	Tufts
1953	Thomas Kelly	Boston University		1981	Greg Shea	Boston College
1954	Gerry Dooling	University of Conn.		1982	William Davis	Babson
1955	David Bell	Dartmouth		1983	Dan McLeod	Springfield St.
1956	George Morse	Tufts		1984	Joseph Miller	Am. Int'l Coll.
1957	Daniel Hurley	Salem State		1985	Steve Kluge	Holy Cross
1958	William Marascalchi	Merrimack College		1986	Chris Brown	U Mass
1959	Len McCarthy	Boston College		1987	Mike Raymond	Univ. of Vt
1960	Charles Moser	Wentworth Tech. Inst.		1988	Thomas Gallagher	Salem State
1961	Joe Andreas	University of Vermont		1989	Kevin Piecewicz	Mass. Maritime
1962	Raymond Rodgers	University of Mass.		1990	Scott Shairs	Bridgewater St
1963	Richard Young	Salem State		1991	Joseph Vaccaro	Salem State
1964	Thomas Lemire	Brown		1992	Michael Cotraro	Mass. Maritime
1965	Joseph Forti	Northeastern U.		1993	Todd Murphy	Tufts
1966	Russell Walsh	Holy Cross		1994	Jason Carlson	St. Michael's
1967	Steve Robbins	Univ. of Colorado		1995	Terry Conant	Plymouth State
1968	John Brewer	Northeastern U.		1996	Pat Heneberry	St. Michael's
1969	Tom Larson	U Mass		1997	Bob Smith	Norwich Univ.
1970	John Hirschfeld	U Mass		1998	David Macdonald	Bowdoin
1971	Jim Modugno	Salem State		1999	Andy Bartlett	Embry-Riddle
1972	Mike Carusi	Tufts		2000	Ryan Hirschfeld	Stoneham

CHARLES A. WALSH SCHOLARSHIP

The Charles A. Walsh Memorial Scholarship is presented to a deserving senior Beverly High School football player each year by the Beverly Football Boosters Sports Club.

Scholarship award recipients are:

1972	Donald Wallace
1973	Robert Frangillo
1974	Brian Nardella
1975	Joe Grein
1976	William Roberts
1977	William Hayes
1978	Mark Boretti
1979	Mike Abate
1980	Chris Kimback
1981	Mark White
1982	Mike Fall
1983	Gary Cowles
1984	Tim Flaherty
1985	Robert Guay
1986	Andrew Morency
1987	Jon Sidman
1988	Jeff Richard
1989	Brett Boretti
1990	Tom Field
1991	Eric Shairs
1992	Paul Grossman
1993	Tom Kaylor
1994	*No Award*
1995	*No Award*
1996	Joel Belmonte
1997	Steve Ward
1998	Mike Goldenberg
1999	Brian Van DeBogert
2000	Pat Belmonte

Jack Heaphy

Jack Heaphy, a member of the Beverly High School class of 1917, played four years of football and was recognized as a pinpoint snapper, a roving center, punt defender and for his ability to read the opposition's plays. The local newspapers reported that Heaphy was one of the best centers playing high school football of his era. A memorable game was against a highly favored Salem team in 1916 in which Jack intercepted a pass and ran it back eighty yards to ensure a Beverly victory. For three years Jack was named All Essex County Interscholastic Center.

In 1917, Jack played football at Georgetown University for one year and after WWI enrolled in Boston College where he played center under Coach Frank Cavanaugh. He was a member of BC's "Team of Destiny" which won the Lambert Trophy and he won distinction as the All American Roving Center.

His coaching career started at Boston College High School in 1923, then to Boston College as a line coach in 1927, and finishing at Dedham High School from 1928 to 1954. He was then appointed Athletic Director serving until his retirement.

In 1948, Jack was named to BC's "All Time Team" and has been inducted into the halls of fame for the Massachusetts High School Coaches (1961), Dedham High (1970), Boston College (1999) and Beverly High (2006).

Jack Heaphy – All-American center at Boston College

Flavio Tosi

After graduating from Beverly High School in 1929, Flavio Tosi went on to Boston College where he distinguished himself as a top college player.

At B.C. he was a leading pass receiver on offense and a hard-hitting defender on defense.

As a senior, he earned and was awarded All-America and All-East honors for his stellar play, which included *ten* quarterback sacks in the Holy Cross game.

Tosi became the first Boston College graduate to play in the National Football League when he signed with the then Boston Redskins after receiving his degree.

He was inducted into the Boston College Varsity Club Athletic Hall of Fame in 1982 and the Beverly High School Athletic Hall of Fame in 2003.

On offense

On defense

A hit on Bronco Nagurski knocked Tosi out cold, but Nagurski later remarked, "I don't think I've ever been hit so hard".

1933

1938

RANTZ L.E.
FIORE F.B.
FROST L.H.B.
QUINN Q.B.
CAPT. BENEDETTI L.G.
ASKMAN C.
RUBIO R.H.B.
DI-CICCO R.G.
MOAR R.T.
OVERBERG L.T.
ROBERTS R.E.
COACH RICHARDSON

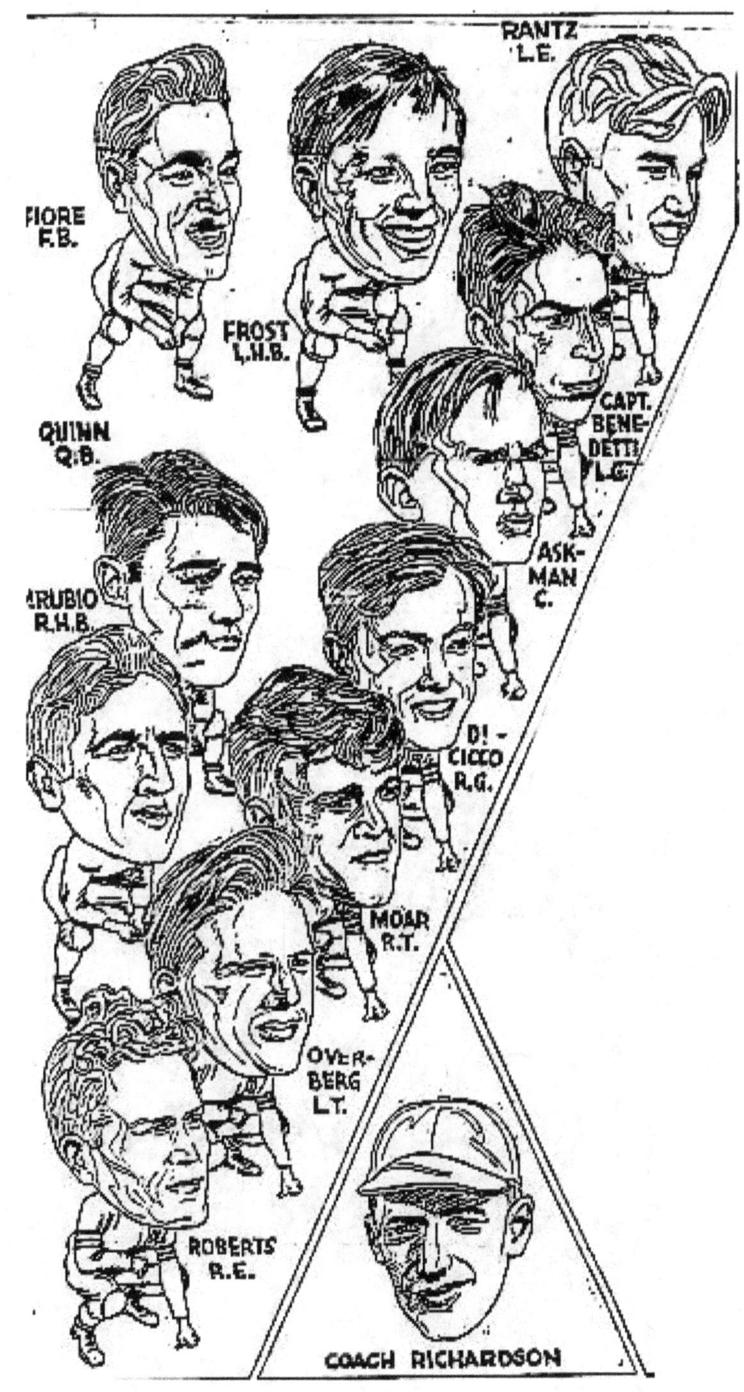

Coach Nick Morris 1940 - 1942

Henry Toczylowski, Head Coach – 1943

Clarence 'Clammy' Foster

'Clammy' worked nights at the 'Shoe' and spent his other waking hours with the boys that played football for Beverly High. There was just no one more dedicated to the well being of the young athletes and he tended their needs for literally decades as he, figuratively, left his blood and his soul right out there on the field.

Walsh Recognition Party

Brother Roberts, Coach Walsh, and Jack Lapsley

1929 – Cheering on their boys

Charlie Pelonzi at St. Anselm College
1933

Coach Charlie Walsh - 1944

Namesake of Hurd Stadium

B. Sumner Hurd
B.H.S. principal, advisor and friend
1904

The 100th Beverly–Salem Game celebration

Seated, from left: Paul Weir, Coach Charlie Pelonzi
Standing, from left: Bob Carr, Norm Pfaff, Coach John Bochynski, Sandy Kessaris,
Leroy 'Red' Hutt, Billy Ransom, Wayne Raymond

1923

Hail, the Conquering Heroes

Beverly 3 - Salem 0
1940

Chick Beaulieu and Aldo Vandi with the Salem goalposts - 1940

Sporting new jerseys and preparing to launch the 1940 season
From left: Enrico Lauranzano, Aldo Vandi, and Frank Bettencourt

1948 All-Star representatives from Beverly

Coach Walsh with, from left, Paul Fraser, Ray LeClerc, Mickey Abate, Billy Ransom
and Sandy Kassaris

On the occasion of their retirement, Charlie Walsh and Charlie Pelonzi are chauffeured by Charlie Manuel, Sr

Front row: Ken Noonan, Peter Connaughton, Vin DiFazio, Tom Roccio, Dennis Gauthier, Myles McPherson, Ron Morse, Phil Carr

Back row: George Stephanos, Dave Markham, George Copelas, Craig Ellis, Jim Corbett

(1950)   Fred Bucci – a life too short

1975

Clowning Around - 1946

Coach Cunningham gets a ride. Hey ! What's going on they were 2 & 8 . . . not 8 & 2 ! However, a victory is a victory and should be rewarded

From left: Gordon Zwicker, Georges Comiskey and Bob Deibner

Typical Halftime

Ya gotta have cheerrleaders

First row, from left: Janice Morency, Barbara Ryan, Grace Him

Back row: Theresa Laverdiere, Pat McLaughlin, 'Chickie' Gadbois, Norma White, Irene Manks

1947

(1999)   Coach Rosinski congratulates Eugene Moore

(1999)   Coach Rosinski instructs Corey Harrington

1914

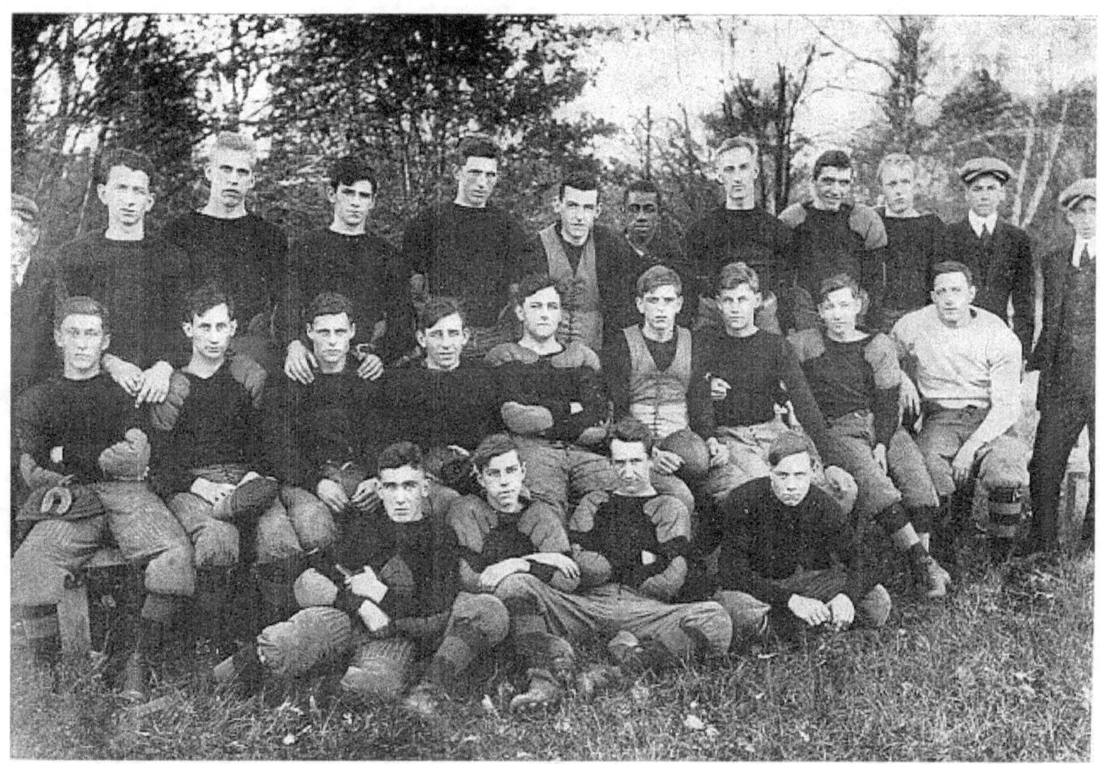

A great picture – too bad we can't identify them all

John Ryan

John Ryan was co-captain of the 1958 Class A undefeated football champions and was All-State First Team in football. He later graduated from the US Naval Academy and played three sports, flew jet planes in the Vietnam war, graduated from Georgetown Law School and later became US Bankruptcy Judge in California where he handled many historic cases.

Peter Abate – Captain 1934

Peter Abate – World famous sculptor - ca. 1990

At Beverly High School, Peter Abate captained the 1934 football team to a successful 7-3-0 season, but his destiny was to leave his mark on the world of art. He was an honors graduate of the School of the Museum of Fine Arts in the late 1930's and went on to become a distinguished sculptor and teacher, winning several national and international awards including the Prix de Rome. In June of 1995, Lizbeth Hall eulogized him with the following, *"He came in through my eyes and through my hands and through my heart. He taught me how to see the form within that stone with my eyes, and how to bring it out of that stone with my hands and most importantly how to give it life with my heart."*

First Row, left to right: Bill Brown (1927*), Leo LeBel (1928), Red Gillis (????)
Second Row: Jack Heaphy (1916), Al Turner (1926), Sam Hansbury (1927), Bob Wiseman (1927)
* Last team year at B.H.S.

Killing time before the 1988 Super Bowl

From left: Head coach Bill Hamor, Assistant coach Roger Rosinski,
Equipment Manager 'Red' Hutt, and Assistant coach Al DiPaolo

A Vignette from 1917

Beverly and Salem played football Thanksgiving day – but the game, instead of being staged on the High School athletic field or on the Bertram field oval at Salem, was played 'somewhere in France.'

This interesting information was gleaned from a letter written to Charles A. Lee by Tom Brady, a former Beverly football star who was, at that time, with the headquarters company of the 101st field artillery 'somewhere in France.'

To allow the holiday to pass without seeing Beverly and Salem in action was evidently too much for the boys – so according to the letter, it was arranged that a game would be played between elevens representing the two cities and the rivalry of nearly a quarter of a century would be perpetuated – even if it would never show up in the records.

How the game came out is blurred in the annals of history and we never knew if the 'orange and black' was triumphant or Salem won even a 'moral victory', but there was satisfaction in the feeling that the holiday did not pass without a game between Beverly and Salem – even if it was played 3000 miles away and, of course, was never honored.

NOTE:

In 1917, Salem cancelled their football season due to World War I and Beverly's Thanksgiving day game was played against Peabody who beat up on our local heroes 20 – 0.

Not to be left out

. Melvin Jeffs

Captain 1925

Herb 'Hubber' Collins

Coach (1926)

Albert Turner

Captain (1926)

Bill Brown

1926

Bill Avery

1926

Wendell Murphy

1926

Ralph Ward

1927

Charlie Pelonzi

1932

Tom Murphy

1935

Bud Malone

1935

Joe DiVincenzo

1935

Laurence Bettencourt

1935

'Lavy' Howard

1935

Harry 'Red' Trowt

1935

Aldo Vandi

1940

Harris Toll

1940

(1955) John Corriveau

(1955) William Gobeille

(1955) Paul Guinivan

(1955) Warner Lund

(1955) Russell Rollins

(1955) Louis Tillson

(1955) David Tosi

(1955) Edward Wallace

(1955) Kenneth Berg

(1955) Anthony Consoli

(1955) Paul MacComisky

(1955) Joseph Palmer

(1955) George Morse

(1955) Alvin Manuel

(1955) Louis Andrews

(1958) Joe Hutchinson

(1958)   Lenny McCarthy   (1958)   Joe Hutchinson   (1958)   Larry McDonnell   (1958)   Jimmy Gibbons

(1958)   Paul Geary   (1958)   Pete Cicchetti   (1958)   Gordon Reid   (1958)   Tom Dooling

(1958)   Leo Allen Connery   (1958)   Joe Starks   (1958)   Bill Hamor   (1958)   Pete

(1958) Tony DiVincenzo   (1958) Jack Mitchell   (1958) Keith Chapman   (1958) Fred Gabriel

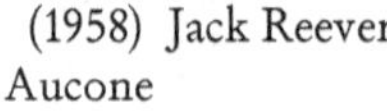

(1958) Jack Reever Aucone

(1958) George Gallagher

(1959) Bill Nisbet

(1959) Don Aucone

(1982) Mike Fall

(1982) Dan MacLeod

Beverly High School, 1875-1928

Beverly High School, 1929-1965

Beverly High School, 1965-Present